Produced in cooperation with The Portland Metropolitan Chamber of Commerce.

The Portland Metropolitan Chamber of Commerce and Community Communications, Inc. would like to express our gratitude to these companies for their leadership in the development of this book.

RUSSELL DEVELOPMENT COMPANY, INC.

SRG Partnership, PC

The Portland Metropolitan Chamber of Commerce and Community Communications, Inc. also would like to thank the following companies for their patronage:

The Bank of Tokyo-Mitsubishi, Ltd., Portland Branch • CADDesign, Inc./www.StateofOregon.com HSBC Bank • Insignia/ESG, Inc. • McDonald Jacobs Accountants and Consultants • PED Manufacturing, Ltd.

Library of Congress Cataloging-in-Publication Data

Portland: portrait of progress / editorial coordinator, Gail Tycer ;
corporate profile writer, Linda Pearson ; feature photographers, Larry
Geddis and Steve Terrill.-- 1st ed.
     p. cm.
   Includes bibliographical references and index.
    ISBN 1-58192-046-6
    1. Portland (Or.)–Civilization. 2. Portland (Or.)–Pictorial works.
3. Portland (Or.)–Economic conditions. 4. Business enterprises–
Oregon–Portland.   I. Tycer, Gail, 1935-   . II. Pearson, Linda, 1955-
. III. Geddis, Larry, 1953-   . IV. Terrill, Steve.
    F884.P85 P67 2001
    979.5'49--dc21   2001004180

Portland

PORTRAIT OF PROGRESS

Editorial coordination by Gail Tycer • Corporate profiles written by Linda Pearson
Featuring the photography of Larry Geddis and Steve Terrill

Portland
PORTRAIT OF PROGRESS

Editorial coordination by Gail Tycer
Corporate profiles written by Linda Scronce-Johnson
Featuring the photography of Larry Geddis
and Steve Terrill

Community Communications, Inc.
Publisher: Ronald P. Beers

Staff of *Portland: Portrait of Progress*
Acquisitions: Henry S. Beers
Publisher's Sales Associate: Marlene Berg
Editor In Chief: Wendi L. Lewis
Managing Editor: Angela C. Johnson
Profile Editor: Mary Catherine Richardson
Design Director: Scott Phillips
Designer: Matt Johnson
Photo Editors: Angela C. Johnson and
Matt Johnson
Contract Manager: Christi Stevens
National Sales Manager: Ronald P. Beers
Sales Assistant: Sandra Akers
Contributing Profile Writer: Jim Dunham
Editorial Assistant: Debra C. Carroll
Acquisitions Coordinator: Angela P. White
Accounting Services: Stephanie Perez
Print Production Manager: Jarrod Stiff
Pre-Press and Separations:
Artcraft Graphic Productions

Community Communications, Inc.
Montgomery, Alabama

David M. Williamson, *Chief Executive Officer*
Ronald P. Beers, *President*
W. David Brown, *Chief Operating Officer*

PHOTO THIS PAGE BY STEVE TERRILL
COVER PHOTO BY LARRY GEDDIS

Table of Contents

Foreword

On behalf of the Portland Metropolitan Chamber of Commerce, I am proud to introduce *Portland: Portrait of Progress*, the second in a series of books spotlighting the unique aspects of Portland and the region.

In just a few short years, Portland has changed dramatically. Our population has grown in both size and ethnic diversity; new office towers dot the skyline; new industries drive our economy; new neighborhoods surround us. Despite the changes, those things that distinguish Portland from other metropolitan areas remain the same—a deep commitment to community, respect for the environment, and a well-planned vision of the future.

When Portland's pioneers incorporated this 640-acre land claim on the Willamette River 150 years ago, they envisioned a world-class port city teeming with prosperous citizens and flourishing trade. Today, Portland's strategic location in the Pacific Northwest and on the Pacific Rim, coupled with our favorable business climate, diverse economic base, and well-educated work force, make Portland extremely attractive to business and industry. Our strong economy and high quality of life—magnificent beauty, profuse recreational activities, excellent schools, and affordable living—make Portland an extraordinary place to live and do business.

Portland: Portrait of Progress is written and photographed by local artists. Their unique perspectives provide insight into the many facets of the region and create a striking image of Portland and the many fine companies that make our community the most livable in the country.

Donald S. McClave
President and Chief Executive Officer
Portland Metropolitan Chamber of Commerce

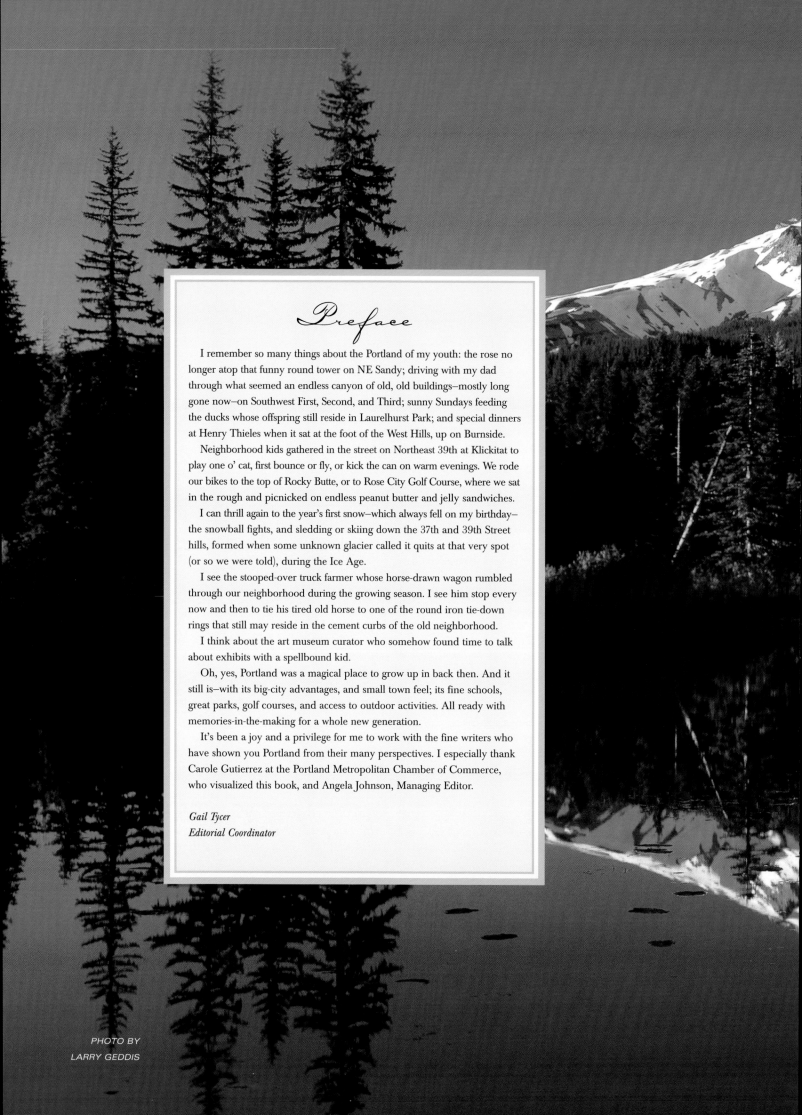

Preface

I remember so many things about the Portland of my youth: the rose no
longer atop that funny round tower on NE Sandy; driving with my dad
through what seemed an endless canyon of old, old buildings—mostly long
gone now—on Southwest First, Second, and Third; sunny Sundays feeding
the ducks whose offspring still reside in Laurelhurst Park; and special dinners
at Henry Thieles when it sat at the foot of the West Hills, up on Burnside.

Neighborhood kids gathered in the street on Northeast 39th at Klickitat to
play one o' cat, first bounce or fly, or kick the can on warm evenings. We rode
our bikes to the top of Rocky Butte, or to Rose City Golf Course, where we sat
in the rough and picnicked on endless peanut butter and jelly sandwiches.

I can thrill again to the year's first snow—which always fell on my birthday—
the snowball fights, and sledding or skiing down the 37th and 39th Street
hills, formed when some unknown glacier called it quits at that very spot
(or so we were told), during the Ice Age.

I see the stooped-over truck farmer whose horse-drawn wagon rumbled
through our neighborhood during the growing season. I see him stop every
now and then to tie his tired old horse to one of the round iron tie-down
rings that still may reside in the cement curbs of the old neighborhood.

I think about the art museum curator who somehow found time to talk
about exhibits with a spellbound kid.

Oh, yes, Portland was a magical place to grow up in back then. And it
still is—with its big-city advantages, and small town feel; its fine schools,
great parks, golf courses, and access to outdoor activities. All ready with
memories-in-the-making for a whole new generation.

It's been a joy and a privilege for me to work with the fine writers who
have shown you Portland from their many perspectives. I especially thank
Carole Gutierrez at the Portland Metropolitan Chamber of Commerce,
who visualized this book, and Angela Johnson, Managing Editor.

Gail Tycer
Editorial Coordinator

PHOTO BY
LARRY GEDDIS

PART
one

PHOTO BY
LARRY GEDDIS

CHAPTER ONE

BY JANN MITCHELL

Portland's Unique Character

This fair City of Roses also could be dubbed an exciting City of Choices.

For choice gave Portland its name in 1851 when Asa Lovejoy and Francis Pettygrove flipped a coin to decide whether this booming new town near the confluence of the Columbia and Willamette Rivers would be Portland or Boston, after cities in their home states.

And, though admittedly different in nature, Portland choices continue today–from where shall we eat–Asian fusion through Tex-Mex, with forty microbreweries tossed into the mix, Portland boasts more restaurants and theaters per capita than any other U.S. city; to where shall we play– the river, mountains, beach; to where shall we shop–the flagship Nike store/athletic museum, an organic grocery, chic boutiques, or funky shops?

Choosing just where to live isn't easy, either! How about a hillside haven with a view of Mount Hood? A floating home bobbing gently on the river? A cozy Sellwood cottage, an Arts and Crafts bungalow in Ladds Addition, a Pearl District loft? Consider a new rowhouse in diverse Northeast, a water-front condo, a city apartment suite, a Nob Hill Victorian.

Portland's unique geography makes skiing on Mount Hood or whale-watching at the coast an equidistant toss-up– reach either destination in just over an hour. If you choose

the beach, pause in nearby Yamhill County for wine-tasting rivaling the Napa Valley–or make a weekend of it, staying at a charming bed and breakfast inn.

Unique may be an overworked word, but surely it was invented for Portland. And yet, for all its high-tech industry, Portland is a down-home place. Neighbors meet–and win City Hall's ear–through neighborhood associations. We cordon off streets for block parties and children's sledding (for that rare two inches of snow). We stage periodic potlucks and progressive dinners (a course in each home). Increasingly popular are community garage sales–grab a map and stroll through maple-shaded neighborhoods to scoop up bargains scattered over driveways and lawns.

Portlanders are civic-minded. We serve as advocates for children in foster care and seniors in nursing homes. Some employers grant us paid time off work to tutor young readers in the SMART (Start Making A Reader Today) program in the Portland School District; and to rebuild and refurbish community facilities and seniors' homes during the United Way of the Columbia-Willamette's Day of Caring. Yearly, some 65,000 volunteers turn out to clean up after parades and keep roadsides, trails, and beaches pristine.

Miss the park trash can in Portland, and it's not unusual for a stranger to pick up the litter for you. Don't be surprised

Unique may be an overworked word, but surely it was invented for Portland.

if you're asked to bring a can of food or a gift for a needy child to a holiday party. And leaning on your car horn will draw stares and even a muttered, "He's obviously not from around here!"

Yet there's an uptown flair to Oregon's largest city, center of a metro population area of nearly two million. Cultural opportunities abound. And getting around town is easy, with transportation choices ranging from taxicabs; to limousines; to the bus; to the MAX light rail, racing to suburban Gresham on the east, to Hillsboro on the west, and eventually to Vancouver, Washington to the north. You can hop a free bus or vintage trolley in Fareless Square to theaters, restaurants, stores, and businesses.

Board a romantic, horse-drawn carriage, or stroll the Transit Mall with sidewalk sculptures, fountains, and

AUTUMN COLOR ADDS TO THE BEAUTY OF THESE VICTORIAN HOMES IN NORTHWEST PORTLAND'S NOB HILL NEIGHBORHOOD. SOME OF THESE HOMES DATE BACK TO 1884, AND ARE ON THE NATIONAL REGISTER OF HISTORIC PLACES. *PHOTO BY LARRY GEDDIS*

flowerbeds. Savor the liveliness of a safe and vibrant downtown, complete with police officers on horseback and bicycle, or pop into one of the ubiquitous Starbucks for a java jolt.

In downtown Portland you can catch a salmon, savor seafood in a floating restaurant, paddle a calm kayak, hop a jet-boat, or board *The Queen of the West*–a Mark Twain-like sternwheeler cruising the Willamette, Columbia, and Snake Rivers.

Come the holidays, Portland literally shines. A giant Christmas tree and a Menorah reign in downtown Pioneer Courthouse Square. The Meier & Frank Christmas Parade the morning after Thanksgiving draws shoppers downtown where carolers sing on street corners. Portland Saturday Market stays open all week long. Lovers of holiday lights drive, walk, and ride horse-drawn wagons past the gaily

decorated homes of Peacock Lane. Brightly-lighted Christmas Ships ply both rivers. And every Portland child's favorite holiday landmark, "Rudolph," with his red nose in neon, flies high above Old Town!

Portland enjoys its diversity, celebrating Chinese New Year in Chinatown, St. Patrick's Day in its Irish pubs, and Cinco de Mayo in Waterfront Park. Later come the Scottish Highland Games, Homowo Festival of African Arts, German Oktoberfest, and festivals with Greek, Italian, Polish, and Scandinavian flavor.

In a state where the governor has been known to sport jeans and cowboy boots no matter the occasion, citizens of the City of Roses dress just as they please. Cashmere and Goretex, lumberjack plaids and Eddie Bauer khakis, designer pumps and hiking boots—you're right in style when you dress your way. Just don't forget your umbrella!

You will notice the greenery-growing rain—some 36 inches a year on average—mostly between October and May. Yet there is sufficient sunshine, with summer temperatures averaging in the 70s, to make gardening a joy.

If you have a taste for the offbeat, Portland provides. The world's smallest park, no larger than a manhole cover. Seals and beavers sporting Christmas wreaths—we just can't resist decorating those downtown Transit Mall sculptures! A volcanic crater in Mount Tabor Park. The world's most prolific pachyderms at the Oregon Zoo. Hollywood and TV movie-making all over town. The actual locations of inspiration for Beverly Cleary's Ramona Quimby children's books—Grant Park and Klickitat Street. And don't miss the 24-Hour Church of Elvis, a shrine to the bizarre.

We're home to the Portland Trail Blazers NBA team, WNBA Portland Fire, Winter Hawks hockey, and Portland Beavers minor league baseball. The old Civic Stadium underwent a major renovation, and re-opened in 2001 as the new PGE Park, home of the Beavers. Get your engine racing at the Portland International Raceway with its June Indy Car event; bet on your favorite horse at Portland Meadows; and cheer for the dogs at Multnomah Greyhound Park. Casinos are an easy drive.

Outdoor activity is a way of life here. Cyclists are protected by designated bike lanes on Portland streets. Runners and walkers regularly commandeer roadsides for dozens of sponsored runs and volk-swalks, or just for a bit of exercise. Snowboarders head for Mount Hood, wind-surfers turn east on the Columbia, hunters and anglers take to nearby fields and streams.

Year-round, Portland is the perfect place to pursue a career, raise a family, savor retirement, and enjoy the outdoors as Mother Nature intended. It's a place and a pace where you can make more than just a good living. You can make a great life.

The choice is yours. ■

TOP: ROW HOUSES IN NORTHWEST PORTLAND'S PEARL DISTRICT. ORIGINALLY A WAREHOUSE DISTRICT, THE AREA IS NOW A THRIVING UPSCALE URBAN NEIGHBORHOOD. *PHOTO BY LARRY GEDDIS* LEFT: THE PARK BLOCKS, RUNNING THROUGH THE CENTER OF PORTLAND'S DOWN-TOWN, WERE INCLUDED IN THE ORIGINAL CITY PLANNING, AND HAVE HISTORICALLY PROVIDED A QUIET PLACE FOR READING OR REFLECTING. *PHOTO BY STEVE TERRILL*

There's an uptown flair to Oregon's largest city of nearly two million. Cultural opportunities abound.

RIGHT: FROM THE PORTLAND BUILDING, A BRONZE PORTLANDIA VIEWS PORTLAND TRANSIT MALL ACTIVITY WITH DETACHED CALM. PORTLAND'S TRANSIT MALL HAS BEEN DESIGNED TO CENTRALIZE BUS TRAFFIC, AND TO PROVIDE A PEOPLE AREA. *PHOTO BY LARRY GEDDIS* FAR RIGHT: THE GATEWAY TO PORTLAND'S CHINATOWN IS A WELL-KNOWN LANDMARK, LEADING TO AUTHENTIC RESTAURANTS AND SHOPS WITHIN PORTLAND'S EARLIEST CHINESE COMMUNITY. *PHOTO BY LARRY GEDDIS*

RIGHT: CREATED BY GEORGIA GERBER IN 1986, ANIMALS IN POOLS ARE BRONZE SCULPTURES ALONG 5TH AND 6TH AVENUES, IN PORTLAND'S DOWNTOWN PIONEER COURTHOUSE AREA. *PHOTO BY LARRY GEDDIS* OPPOSITE PAGE: HISTORIC PORTLAND BUILDINGS DISPLAY AN UNUSUAL NUMBER OF IN-PLACE CAST IRON ARCHITECTURAL FEATURES, MAKING THE CITY A "MUST SEE" FOR ARCHITECTURE ENTHUSIASTS. *PHOTO BY STEVE TERRILL*

AZALEAS AND
RHODODENDRONS
THRIVE AMONG ONE
SUBURBAN GARDEN
WHILE COLORFUL IRIS
BLOOM ALONG A
FENCE BORDERING
SUMMERLAKE PARK,
CENTERPIECE OF A
SUBURBAN TIGARD
FAMILY NEIGHBORHOOD.
PHOTOS BY
STEVE TERRILL

This fair City of Roses also could be dubbed an exciting City of Choices.

PORTLANDERS LOVE FLOWERS, AND THE CITY'S MILD CLIMATE ENCOURAGES COLORFUL FLOWER DISPLAYS THROUGHOUT THE YEAR. *PHOTOS BY STEVE TERRILL*

Outdoor activity is a way of life here.

PORTLAND IS MADE FOR
OUTDOOR FESTIVALS.
ALMOST EVERY
WEEKEND DURING THE
WARM MONTHS SEES A
SPECIAL CELEBRATION
SOMEWHERE IN THE
CITY, LIKE THIS ITALIAN
FESTIVAL IN DOWNTOWN
PIONEER SQUARE. *PHOTO
BY LARRY GEDDIS*

LEFT AND BOTTOM LEFT: PORTLAND SATURDAY MARKET, ALSO OPEN ON SUNDAY, IS PART STREET FAIR, PART ART GALLERY, AND ALL FUN! *PHOTOS BY STEVE TERRILL* BOTTOM RIGHT: KIDS LOVE CELEBRATIONS! THESE CHILDREN ENJOY PERFORMING AT THE POLISH FESTIVAL. *PHOTO BY STEVE TERRILL*

RIGHT: A CARPENTER GOTHIC CLASSIC FROM PORTLAND'S EARLY DAYS, THE OLD CHURCH IS NOW A PLACE WHERE PEOPLE GATHER TO HEAR GOOD MUSIC, GOOD SPEAKERS, AND TO PARTICIPATE IN COMMUNITY ACTIVITIES. *PHOTO BY STEVE TERRILL* FAR RIGHT: LOCATED ON PORTLAND'S NAITO PARKWAY, MILL ENDS PARK WAS NAMED FOR THE MYTHICAL PARK CREATED BY *OREGON JOURNAL* EDITORIAL WRITER AND COLUMNIST DICK FAGAN. REPUTED TO BE THE WORLD'S SMALLEST, MILL ENDS PARK ENCOMPASSES 24 SQUARE INCHES. *PHOTO BY LARRY GEDDIS* OPPOSITE PAGE: FOR MORE THAN 100 YEARS, ST. JAMES LUTHERAN CHURCH HAS SURVEYED THE PARK BLOCKS FROM THE SOUTHWEST CORNER OF PARK AND JEFFERSON IN DOWN-TOWN PORTLAND. DEDICATED TO SERVING THE NEEDS OF PEOPLE LIVING AND WORKING IN THE DOWNTOWN COMMUNITY, ST. JAMES PROVIDES FULL-TIME DAY CARE FOR CHILDREN, A FOOT CARE CLINIC FOR THE ELDERLY AND DIS-ABLED, SCHOLARSHIPS, EDUCATIONAL PROGRAMS, AND AFFORDABLE HOUSING FOR DOWNTOWN RESIDENTS. *PHOTO BY STEVE TERRILL*

"Portland's downtown is the envy of most other American cities. It's a true 24-hour city, with wonderful places to work, to live, to eat, to shop—and it's the center of cultural activities. Our downtown reflects the pride of the members of our community."

John W. Russell
President
Russell Development Company, Inc.

EARLY PORTLAND BUILDER DAVID COLE BUILT WHAT IS NOW THE QUEEN ANNE MANSION IN 1885 FOR HIS BRIDE, AMANDA LAURA BOONE, GREAT GRANDDAUGHTER OF DANIEL BOONE. ITS NORTH PORTLAND GARDEN NOW FEATURES MILLIONS OF TINY TWINKLING LIGHTS DURING WEDDINGS, HOLIDAYS, AND CELEBRATIONS OF ALL KINDS. *PHOTO BY LARRY GEDDIS*

WHEN THE WHITE STAG STARTS SPORTING A RED NOSE, IT'S HOLIDAY SEASON IN PORTLAND! DESIGNATED AS A PORTLAND CITY LANDMARK, THE ORIGINAL SIGN DATES TO 1927, WHEN IT FEATURED AN OUTLINE OF THE STATE OF OREGON. THE WHITE STAG COMPANY ADDED THE "REINDEER" IN 1959, AND IN 1996 THE SIGN WAS ACQUIRED BY MADE IN OREGON STORES, WHICH HAVE CONTINUED THIS HOLIDAY TRADITION. *PHOTO BY LARRY GEDDIS*

Come the holidays, Portland literally shines.

THE CHRISTMAS FLEET—
A MAGNIFICENT FLOTILLA
OF BRIGHTLY-LIGHTED
BOATS PARADING UP
AND DOWN THE
COLUMBIA AND
WILLAMETTE RIVERS
EACH NIGHT DURING
THE HOLIDAY SEASON—
IS A LONG-STANDING
HOLIDAY TRADITION.
PHOTO BY LARRY GEDDIS

CHAPTER TWO

BY MAGGI WHITE

What There Is to Do

"MOST CHERISHED IN THIS MUNDANE WORLD IS A PLACE WITHOUT TRAFFIC; TRULY IN THE MIDST OF A CITY THERE CAN BE MOUNTAIN AND FOREST." WEN ZHENGMING (1470-1559) THE CLASSICAL CHINESE GARDEN OF AWAKENING ORCHIDS, THE LARGEST AUTHENTIC URBAN SUZHOU-STYLE GARDEN EVER CREATED OUTSIDE CHINA, IS SUCH A PLACE, AND IS FOUND RIGHT IN THE MIDDLE OF THE BUSTLING CITY OF PORTLAND. THIS HAND-MADE DRAGON TYPIFIES THE DETAIL TO BE FOUND ON THE GARDEN'S NINE PAVILIONS AND BUILDINGS. *PHOTO BY LARRY GEDDIS*

The day started out like many others, with an invitation to dine at a Thai restaurant that made the cover of *Bon Appetit.* While the table of six tasted stunningly presented morsels in the hotel dining room, in the lounge the sensuous sound of a tenor saxophone with a jazz combo played to an attentive, standing room only audience.

Outside, like a scene from a movie, stretch limos slowly moved out of focus, and a horse and buggy took a newly-wed couple on a romantic ride, clip-clopping down Southwest Broadway. Think you see New York in this picture? Is that your final answer? Wrong. We're talking about downtown Portland.

Whether it's a small ethnic restaurant in one of the city neighborhoods or dessert and ice cream in an old house where musicians often come in and play at unpredictable hours of the evening, this is a city where discovering something new in all areas is highly enjoyable and ever changing.

There is live music somewhere in the city every night of the week. Many musicians make Portland their home and can be found playing in the city's lively club scene, where jazz, especially, has several venues. If jazz isn't your interest, you can go ballroom dancing or learn how to line dance. Clubs for the eighteen–and–older crowd are neighborly places, and clubs on the wilder side are indicative of Portlanders' independent spirit.

Portland is amazingly lacking in pretentious attitude. It's a small town with Midwestern hospitality, a high quality of life, and a relatively inexpensive cost of living. It's a city of lighted bridges, the shimmering Willamette River separating east from west, and an awesome skyline at night. Fishermen explore the river, and pleasure boats pull up to riverfront eateries for fish and chips or a bottle of beer. Portland is a city to be explored to the fullest.

Portland is a unique city of contrasts. Quiet places like the Crystal Springs Rhododendron Garden–one of Portland's many public gardens, and the Roman Catholic Grotto offer a place for calm and contemplation as counterpoint to the bustle of a thriving city.

There's plenty to do for families, whether thrilling to rides or roller skating at Oaks Park, or going on outings to Alpenrose Dairy, whose grounds host world-class youth athletic events along with its Dairyville fun. The Oregon Museum of Science and Industry is one of the nation's top science museums, with hundreds of interactive exhibits and hands-on demonstrations, as well as a big screen OMNIMAX theater, the Northwest's largest planetarium, and the USS *Blueback*, the most modern U.S. submarine on public display in North America.

The Children's Museum not only entertains children age ten–and–younger with hands-on exhibits, but it's a place

OPPOSITE PAGE: FOUR GENERATIONS OF PORTLAND CHILDREN HAVE SKATED AT "THE OAKS," AND THRILLED TO THE RIDES AT OAKS PARK IN SOUTHEAST PORTLAND. CENTERPIECE OF THIS HISTORIC AMUSEMENT PARK IS ITS NEWLY-REFURBISHED, OCTOGENARIAN CAROUSEL—ONE OF FEWER THAN 200 STILL OPERATING IN THE COUNTRY. *PHOTO BY LARRY GEDDIS*

This is a city where discovering something new in all areas is highly enjoyable and ever changing.

where their mothers can visit with friends, and find adult conversation. The Museum's new home is in Washington Park, across from the Oregon Zoo, famous for its highly successful Asian elephant-breeding program—the most-visited paid attraction in the state. Only Multnomah Falls in the spectacular Columbia Gorge, and Timberline Lodge on beautiful Mount Hood, attract more visitors. Each is about an hour from Portland, and each is free. Near the zoo are the lovely traditional Japanese Garden and the world-famous International Rose Test Garden, both so high in Portland's West Hills you also can enjoy a panoramic city view.

Visit the Portland Classical Chinese Garden, near the river in Northwest Portland, the largest urban classical Chinese garden in the country. Then visit Portland's historic Chinatown for *dim sum* at one of its excellent restaurants.

The city's thriving arts scene opens with a bang in the fall. Beautiful balls and dinners attract the smart set, hailing the new season for the Oregon Ballet Theatre, Oregon Symphony, and Portland Opera, as well as the newly renovated Portland Art Museum, which attracts international shows.

The cultural scene includes the wonderfully restored historic downtown library; the Northwest Film & Video School; a new campus for the Northwest College of Art; and photography, art, and antique galleries. Art is still a bargain in Oregon.

Portland is also home to the Oregon College of Art and Craft, and the Portland Institute for Contemporary Art, both nationally recognized. Every year, more than l,000 artists and arts organizations benefit from the Regional Arts and Culture Council grants and technical assistance services. The city plays host each year to the Portland Creative Conference, which attracts film people from all over the world.

Numerous independent bookstores sell everything from cookbooks to mystery novels. There are more than a dozen innovative, venturesome dance groups, and some fifty choral groups, many of them open to new members. The popular Chamber Music Northwest offers a fine counterpoint to the annual Jazz Festival.

Even with so much going on, Portland is also a museum city. You'll find museums offering historical, cultural, and environmental insights, along with the nation's only advertising museum.

On the retail side, Portland is the home of Nike and adidas, Saks Fifth Avenue and Nordstrom. Portland Saturday Market in Old Town is a must-do. Go to Northwest 23rd Avenue, a lively, people-oriented area of unique boutiques, restaurants, and coffee houses–the place to people-watch, as well as to shop. Antique shops and off-beat and classical dining characterize the Sellwood area. Or try The Pearl, with its lofts, art galleries, antique shops, and one-of-a-kind restaurants.

Portlanders enjoy the outdoors. Virtually every week during the summer months will find festivals in the city's many parks. The Portland Rose Festival is an early summer tradition, with events ranging from coronations and parades to car races and an air show, lasting several weeks into the summer. Within thirty minutes of Portland you can be sipping wine at McMinnville's annual wine festival, or at one of the many award-winning wineries in the valley.

AUGUST IN PORTLAND BRINGS THE BITE: A TASTE OF PORTLAND TO WATERFRONT PARK. THIS ANNUAL THREE-DAY FESTIVAL FEATURES GREAT MUSIC AND GREAT FOOD FROM MORE THAN TWENTY OF THE CITY'S FAVORITE RESTAURANTS TO BENEFIT THE SPECIAL OLYMPICS OREGON.
PHOTO BY LARRY GEDDIS

HELD EACH JUNE AS A
PART OF THE PORTLAND
ROSE FESTIVAL, THE
TIGARD FESTIVAL OF
BALLOONS IS HELD AT
COOK PARK IN TIGARD.
PHOTO BY LARRY GEDDIS

Virtually every week during the summer months will find festivals in the city's many parks.

THE PORTLAND-KAOHSIUNG SISTER CITY ASSOCIATION DRAGON BOAT RACES ON THE WILLAMETTE RIVER ADD COLOR TO PORTLAND'S ANNUAL JUNE ROSE FESTIVAL. *PHOTO BY LARRY GEDDIS*

Walking is pure joy in the lovely downtown Park Blocks behind Portland State University, where 17,000 students come to study every day. The Salmon Street Springs at Tom McCall Waterfront Park attracts numerous families who come to watch their children play in its refreshing waters on hot days.

When it comes to sports, to many the Blazers are THE game in town. The team is regularly a serious contender for an NBA championship, and fiercely loyal fans fill the Rose Garden to cheer them on. Portland also has a Women's NBA team, the Portland Fire, an expansion team of players who draw summer crowds. Portland's Winter Hawks keep hockey fans on their toes.

Recapturing the nostalgia of a vintage baseball park, the $38.5 million renovation of Civic Stadium, now PGE Park, also provides a home for the variety of family-friendly sports and entertainment events that add to the city's vitality.

With so much to see and do, this remarkable city of diversity and contrast truly has something for everyone. ■

THOUSANDS OF MILK CARTONS ARE TRANSFORMED INTO RACING VESSELS WITH GLUE, STAPLES, AND TAPE FOR THE PORTLAND ROSE FESTIVAL MILK CARTON BOAT RACES, HELD EACH JUNE AT THE WESTMORELAND PARK CASTING POND. *PHOTO BY LARRY GEDDIS*

With so much to see and do, this remarkable city of diversity and contrast truly has something for everyone.

THE HAWTHORNE BRIDGE AND THE NIGHTLIGHTS OF THE PORTLAND SKYLINE ARE REFLECTED IN THE PEACEFUL WILLAMETTE RIVER. *PHOTO BY LARRY GEDDIS*

"Each of the Doubletree hotels in the city of Portland offers a unique variety of dining and entertainment excursions. Whether local citizens are looking for a weekend getaway or visitors from around the world are seeking to explore our magnificent city, our accommodations are world class. Portland offers a variety of things to see and do and the Doubletree is proud to play host to those interested in learning more about our home. Come stay with us and let us proudly show you what we're all about!"

Doug Heaton
General Manager
Doubletree Hotels

THE PEPSI WATERFRONT VILLAGE AT WATERFRONT PARK IS AN ANNUAL HIGHLIGHT OF PORTLAND'S ROSE FESTIVAL CELEBRATION. SHIPS FROM THE U.S. NAVY AND EVEN FROM OTHER COUNTRIES TIE UP ALONG THE SEAWALL AND INVITE VISITORS ABOARD. *PHOTO BY LARRY GEDDIS*

Quiet places offer calm and contemplation
as counterpoint to the bustle of a thriving city.

CATHEDRAL PARK IS LOCATED UNDER THE ST. JOHN'S BRIDGE IN NORTH PORTLAND. BUILT IN 1931, THE ST. JOHN'S BRIDGE IS THE ONLY STEEL SUSPENSION BRIDGE IN THE CITY, AND ONE OF JUST THREE IN THE STATE. *PHOTO BY STEVE TERRILL*

HIGH ABOVE DOWN-
TOWN PORTLAND IN THE
CITY'S SCENIC WEST
HILLS, WASHINGTON
PARK'S JAPANESE
GARDEN PROVIDES A
TRANQUIL HAVEN IN A
BUSTLING CITY. *PHOTO
STEVE TERRILL*

PORTLAND'S JAPANESE
GARDEN FEATURES FIVE
TRADITIONAL GARDEN
STYLES. HERE, AZALEAS
LINE THE STEPS LEADING
THROUGH THE NATURAL
GARDEN. *PHOTO BY
LARRY GEDDIS*

THE ROSE CITY'S
WORLD-FAMOUS
INTERNATIONAL ROSE
TEST GARDENS OVER-
LOOK THE CITY SKYLINE
FROM THE WEST HILLS,
WITH MOUNT HOOD,
AN HOUR OR SO AWAY
FROM THE CITY, VISIBLE
IN THE DISTANCE. THE
GARDENS ARE LOCATED
IN WASHINGTON PARK,
WHICH IS NESTLED
BETWEEN PORTLAND
HEIGHTS NEIGHBOR-
HOODS AND PROVIDES
AN AMAZING VARIETY OF
ACTIVITY AND ENDLESS
SURPRISES—FROM
SCENIC OUTLOOKS, TO
FORMAL GARDENS, TO
THE ZOO, TO MILES OF
HIKING TRAILS. *PHOTO
BY LARRY GEDDIS*

PORTLAND'S MANY
PUBLIC GARDENS INCLUDE
THE HISTORIC COLLEC-
TION OF THE NATURALIZED
LEACH BOTANICAL
GARDEN IN THE SOUTH-
EAST PORTION OF THE
CITY. THIS TRANQUIL
COURTYARD FOUNTAIN IS
PART OF THE FORMER
HOME OF LILLA LEACH,
RENOWNED BOTANIST,
AND HER PHARMACIST
HUSBAND JOHN, WHO
GAVE THEIR ESTATE TO
THE CITY OF PORTLAND.
OWNER OF ONE OF THE
LARGEST PHARMACIES IN
THE COUNTRY AT THE
TIME, JOHN KEPT HIS
PROMISE TO TAKE LILLA
WHERE "CAKE-EATING
BOTANISTS" WOULD
NOT GO. *PHOTO BY
LARRY GEDDIS*

SPRINGTIME MEANS A
WALK THROUGH THE
CRYSTAL SPRINGS
RHODODENDRON
GARDEN IN SOUTHEAST
PORTLAND. A SPRING-FED
LAKE, WOODED ISLAND,
AND PENINSULA ARE
PART OF THE SEVEN AND
ONE-HALF ACRE GARDEN,
WHICH DISPLAYS
THOUSANDS OF AZALEAS
AND RHODODENDRONS.
PHOTO BY LARRY GEDDIS

RIGHT: THE ROSE WATER SCULPTURE RISES 80 FEET FROM THE CONCOURSE ROTUNDA OF PIONEER PLACE IN DOWNTOWN PORTLAND. THE SHOPPING AREA COMPLETED A MAJOR EXPANSION IN THE SPRING OF 2000. *PHOTO BY LARRY GEDDIS*

FAR RIGHT:PASSENGERS BOARD THE RESTORED HISTORIC WILLAMETTE SHORE TROLLEY AT RIVERPLACE STATION TO TAKE A SCENIC RIDE ALONG THE WILLAMETTE RIVER TO LAKE OSWEGO. *PHOTO BY LARRY GEDDIS*

RIVERPLACE IS AN URBAN RESORT WITH A MARINA, HOTEL, RESTAURANTS, SHOPS, AND CONDOMINIUMS IN THE HEART OF DOWNTOWN. *PHOTO BY LARRY GEDDIS*

OPPOSITE PAGE: TAKE A STERNWHEELER THROUGH THE HEART OF PORTLAND DOWN THE WILLAMETTE RIVER. SUMMERTIME NARRATED CRUISES DEPART FROM DOWNTOWN WATERFRONT PARK. *PHOTO BY LARRY GEDDIS*

RIGHT: THE PROCESSION OF THE SPECIES, PORTLAND'S LARGEST EARTH DAY EVENT, FEATURES MARCHERS, COSTUMED TO REPRESENT AIR, WATER, AND ENDANGERED ANIMALS, IN A COLORFUL PROCESSION THROUGH DOWNTOWN PORTLAND. *PHOTO BY LARRY GEDDIS*

RIGHT & TOP RIGHT: THE ANNUAL DOGGIE DASH BRINGS OUT DOG OWNERS OF ALL AGES, WITH THEIR DOGS OF ALL SIZES AND BREEDS. STARTING ALONG SOUTHWEST NAITO PARKWAY, AND ENDING IN WATERFRONT PARK, THIS TWO-MILE FUN RUN AND WALK RAISES MONEY FOR THE OREGON HUMANE SOCIETY. *PHOTOS BY LARRY GEDDIS*

OPPOSITE PAGE: ONE OF THE MOST POPULAR EXHIBITS AT THE OREGON ZOO IN PORTLAND'S SOUTHWEST HILLS IS LORIKEET LANDING. VISITORS CAN FEED NECTAR TO THESE VERY SOCIAL AUSTRALIAN PARROTS. *PHOTO BY LARRY GEDDIS*

Portland is a city to be explored to the fullest.

LOCATED ALONG THE EAST BANK OF THE WILLAMETTE RIVER, THE OREGON MUSEUM OF SCIENCE AND INDUSTRY (OMSI) FEATURES OUTSTANDING EXHIBITS, AND A WIDE RANGE OF PROGRAMS FOR CHILDREN, FAMILIES, AND ADULTS. THE U.S. SUBMARINE MEMORIAL, THE USS *BLUEBACK*, IS DEDICATED TO THE MEMORY OF SHIPMATES WHO GAVE THEIR LIVES WHILE SERVING IN THE SUBMARINE FLEET. *PHOTO BY LARRY GEDDIS*

OCCUPYING AN ENTIRE CITY BLOCK, GARDEN OF AWAKENING ORCHIDS IS A UNIQUE FRIENDSHIP PROJECT THAT EVOLVED FROM PORTLAND'S STRONG SISTER CITY RELATIONSHIP WITH SUZHOU, CHINA. AT THE CENTER OF THIS PEACE-FUL CLASSICAL CHINESE GARDEN IS ITS 8,000-SQUARE-FOOT BRIDGED LAKE, WHOSE WATERS SUGGEST MYSTERY AND ENCOURAGE INNER PEACE. *PHOTO BY LARRY GEDDIS*

TOP: PORTLAND'S HISTORIC PITTOCK MANSION WAS BUILT IN 1914 FOR PORTLAND PIONEERS HENRY AND GEORGIANA PITTOCK. ARRIVING "BAREFOOT AND PENNILESS" IN 1853 AFTER TRAVELING THE OREGON TRAIL TO PORTLAND, HENRY WORKED AS A PRINTER'S DEVIL ON THE WEEKLY *OREGONIAN* NEWSPAPER, SLEEPING ON A COT UNDER THE COUNTER. BY 1860, HE TOOK OWNERSHIP OF WHAT IS NOW PORTLAND'S *OREGONIAN* NEWSPAPER, AND WENT ON TO BUILD AN EMPIRE INCORPORATING REAL ESTATE, BANKING, RAILROADS, STEAMBOATS, SHEEP RANCHING, SILVER MINING, AND THE PULP AND PAPER INDUSTRY. GEORGIANA DEDICATED HERSELF TO CIVIC ACTIVITIES. THE HOUSE IS NOW OPEN TO THE PUBLIC. *PHOTO BY STEVE TERRILL*

BOTTOM: ACROSS FROM THE OREGON ZOO IN PORTLAND'S WEST HILLS, THE WORLD FORESTRY CENTER FEATURES MEETING SPACE, AND MANY PERMANENT AND CHANGING EXHIBITS. *PHOTO BY LARRY GEDDIS*

HOME OF THE PORTLAND TRAIL BLAZERS NBA PROFESSIONAL BASKETBALL TEAM, THE 19,000-SEAT ROSE GARDEN MULTI-PURPOSE ARENA SITS ON THE EAST SIDE OF THE WILLAMETTE RIVER. THE ROSE GARDEN ARENA ALSO INCLUDES MEMORIAL COLISEUM, AN ENTERTAINMENT COMPLEX, AND A PUBLIC PLAZA. *PHOTO BY STEVE TERRILL*

PORTLAND'S FIERCELY LOYAL TRAIL BLAZER FANS REGULARLY FILL THE ROSE GARDEN TO CHEER THEIR FAVORITE NBA CONTENDER. *PHOTO COURTESY OF PORTLAND TRAIL BLAZERS*

ONE OF THE MOST
EXCITING TEAMS IN THE
WESTERN HOCKEY
LEAGUE, THE PORTLAND
WINTER HAWKS IS
ALWAYS A CONTENDER.
*PHOTO BY BOB
BECHTOLD/COURTESY
OF PORTLAND
WINTER HAWKS*

BOTTOM LEFT AND
RIGHT: HOME OF THE
PACIFIC COAST LEAGUE
PORTLAND BEAVERS
BASEBALL TEAM, PGE
PARK RECAPTURES THE
NOSTALGIA OF A VINTAGE
BASEBALL PARK. THE
PORTLAND TIMBERS A
LEAGUE SOCCER TEAM
ALSO PLAYS HERE.
RENOVATION OF THE OLD
CIVIC STADIUM WAS
COMPLETED IN 2001 AT A
COST OF $38.5 MILLION,
AND NOW PROVIDES A
GATHERING PLACE FOR A
VARIETY OF FAMILY-
FRIENDLY SPORTS
AND ENTERTAINMENT.
*PHOTOS BY
LARRY GEDDIS*

CHAPTER THREE

BY STUART WATSON

Outdoors & Recreation

A KAYAKER NAVIGATES
OVER CARTER FALLS ON
THE WILD AND SCENIC
UPPER CLACKAMAS
RIVER, IN OREGON'S
MT. HOOD NATIONAL
FOREST. *PHOTO BY
LARRY GEDDIS*

It's 9 A.M. on a sunny Saturday in September.

On the flanks of 11,239-foot Mount Hood, several novice climbers learn the ropes on Whitewater Glacier.

Thousands of feet below, nature photographer Adam Bacher follows the trail above 620-foot Multnomah Falls, the second highest in the United States.

Below and a few miles west toward the city of Portland, windsurfers whip across the Columbia River for spectators staring down from Crown Point.

Around the bend, neurologist Kirk Weller finds quiet time, guiding his thoughts and kayak down the rapids of the Clackamas River.

In the heart of Portland itself, Annette Cantu and teammates dig their paddles into the Willamette River, and their national-class dragon boat surges forward.

Beyond the city's skyscrapers, Caroline Petrich steps briskly through the early fall leaves of the nation's largest forested urban park, trying to keep pace with her dog, Tabouli.

And less than two hours' drive west, Kim Rueter hops to her feet and slides down the face of a wave surging toward the Oregon shore.

So it goes, from east to west, as the residents of the Portland metropolitan area take advantage of outdoor attractions that, to many minds, make Portland one of the most livable cities in North America.

For sheer diversity of outdoor recreation, few cities can boast as much to offer as Portland. Where else can residents in a single summer day catch snowboard air off a half-pipe at the 8,450-foot Palmer Snowfield on Mount Hood, hit an afternoon windsurfing session in the Columbia River Gorge, the sport's summertime world capital, and still have time for a warm-down mountain bike ride at sunset through the city's 5,000-acre Forest Park?

Or maybe their preferences run to golf and tennis. Dozens of public and private courses offer golfers as much or as little challenge as they could want. "With quality golf courses, excellent weather, and wonderful community support, Portland has been discovered," says Jim Gibbons, executive director of the Oregon Golf Association.

A frequent host to major USGA tournaments, Portland benefits from a mild Pacific Northwest climate. With little snow and regular natural irrigation–OK, it's rain, but just enough–the city's courses invite serious golfers to polish their game all year round.

Scores of courses welcome the public. Not to single out any course, but simply for illustration, Gibbons noted that the Pumpkin Ridge Golf Club west of the city is a marvelous course for the overall quality of its experience.

"The shot values are good, the quality of the holes is wonderful, the ambiance is great," he says.

OPPOSITE PAGE:
WILLAMETTE MISSION
STATE PARK, BETWEEN
PORTLAND AND SALEM,
PROVIDES A VARIETY OF
YEAR-ROUND OUTDOOR
ACTIVITIES. *PHOTO BY
STEVE TERRILL*

For sheer diversity of outdoor recreation, few cities can boast as much to offer as Portland.

The city parks bureau owns and operates five 18-hole courses. *Golf Digest* magazine has rated the Eastmoreland Golf Course among the top 25 nationally, and the Heron Lakes Golf Course among the top 75 public courses in the country.

To be sure, the city's park system supports more than golf. With 9,714 acres of parks, gardens, sports fields, recreation sites, and open spaces in some 590 locations, residents can pick their play. From tennis to volleyball, from soccer to softball, the facilities require only a willing user. The parks bureau sponsors a host of organized activities, everything from team sports for children and adults, to nature hikes and field trips inside the city and to destinations beyond.

For hikers and climbers of a hardier sort, Portland…well, rocks. John Godino, speaking for the Portland-based Mazamas climbing club, notes that residents have access within a three-hour drive to some of the most challenging and varied hiking and climbing terrain in the world.

TOP: CROWN POINT, ON THE OREGON SIDE OF THE COLUMBIA RIVER GORGE, COMMANDS A SPECTACULAR VIEW OF THIS INCREDIBLE ICE-AGE PHENOMENON, LESS THAN AN HOUR FROM THE CITY. *PHOTO BY LARRY GEDDIS*

RIGHT: A BIG LEAF MAPLE TREE IN AUTUMN SPLENDOR FRAMES A FARM IN THE COLUMBIA RIVER GORGE NATIONAL SCENIC AREA— A FAVORITE SUNDAY DRIVE. *PHOTO BY STEVE TERRILL*

OPPOSITE PAGE: WILLAMETTE RIVER BACKWATER PROVIDES A PLACE TO FISH, AND TO DREAM. *PHOTO BY STEVE TERRILL*

A COUNTRY HOME
EMERGES FROM A
FOGGY AUTUMN
MORNING IN RURAL
MULTNOMAH COUNTY.
COUNTRY LIVING CAN BE
AN EASY COMMUTE TO
THE CITY. *PHOTO BY
STEVE TERRILL*

EARLY MORNING FOG
CREATES A MYSTICAL
SIGHT IN RURAL
MULTNOMAH COUNTY,
MINUTES FROM THE
CITY'S CENTER. *PHOTO
BY STEVE TERRILL*

Mount Hood, the dominant feature of the city's eastern skyline, attracts more climbers than any other peak in the world except Japan's Mount Fuji. To the north, climbers also have the option of tackling 12,307-foot Mount Adams or going to the heart of North America's signature geologic event from the last two decades—the eruption on May 18, 1980, of Mount St. Helens.

Now the center of the 110,000-acre Mount St. Helens National Volcanic Monument, Mount St. Helens invites casual visitors, backcountry campers, mountain bikers, and climbers. It's just one of a dozen wilderness areas within easy driving distance of Portland, among them the 105,600-acre Goat Rocks Wilderness, and 47,270-acre Mount Adams Wilderness in southern Washington; and the 46,520-acre Mount Hood, and 44,560-acre Salmon-Huckleberry areas in Oregon.

"Bird Creek Meadows on the southeast slope of Mount Adams has the most incredible wildflowers in late August," says Adam Bacher, who has hiked throughout the West in search of subject matter for his dramatic landscape photos. "And yet, in Portland, you can go to Lower Macleay Park, and the trail goes along a really pretty stream, and right there, you feel like you're out in the wilderness."

Any one trail affords the fit and persistent hiker a number of stunning views.

OREGON'S TALLEST WATERFALL, SPECTACULAR MULTNOMAH FALLS, PLUNGES 620 FEET INTO THE COLUMBIA RIVER GORGE. VISITORS MAY ALSO ENJOY DINING AT THE HISTORIC STONE DAY LODGE. *PHOTO BY LARRY GEDDIS*

For people seeking a close-in day hike, nothing quite compares with the Columbia River Gorge National Scenic Area. Stretching east of Portland for eighty miles, the protected area straddles the second largest river in the United States. Towering basalt bluffs rise more than 4,000 feet on either side, and from the tops of those bluffs fall the greatest concentration of waterfalls in the Northwest.

Dozens of trails wind up the bluffs, and any one trail affords the fit and persistent hiker a number of stunning views up and down the only river to slice completely through the Cascade Range. Each spring, for instance, hikers by the hundreds flock to the summit of Dog Mountain for the scenery and dramatic wildflower blooms.

From the slopes of the region's volcanic peaks flow icy-cold streams, perfect for the salmon and steelhead trout that call them home, and just as perfect for the anglers and kayakers who choose to ply their skills in the plunging rapids.

"Kayakers around the world perk right up when they think about kayaking here," says Kirk Weller, a native of Colorado, but devoted now to Northwest waters. "You can boat ten out of the twelve months around here, and the Deschutes and White Salmon can even be boated year-round."

Armed instead with fishing rods, Portland residents can cast a line in the nearby waters of the Clackamas and Sandy Rivers, or drive two hours to the fish-rich waters of Central Oregon or the Oregon Coast. A variety of migratory fish runs keep anglers busy all year.

The snowfields of Mount Hood, in their own fashion, cast a magic spell on skiers and snowboarders during all four seasons. With five ski areas—including Mount Hood Ski Bowl, the largest night skiing area in North America, and the 2,159-acre Mount Hood Meadows Ski Area—Mount Hood has something for everyone.

Only one of those areas, however, runs all twelve months, and because it does, thousands of die-hard snowboarders flock to the Timberline Lodge Ski Area each summer to carve snow and air from the sculpted spines, hips, rollers, table tops, and half- and quarter-pipes of the Palmer Snowfield. A freelance graphic designer in Portland, Kim Rueter, loves to snowboard. But when everyone else is heading to the hills, she and husband Bob head west two hours to some of Oregon's best surfing beaches.

"When it's nice and sunny on Mount Hood, it's just the same at the beach," Rueter says. "Except that we're out in the sun, and we've got it all to ourselves." ∎

TOP: TODAY, MOUNTAIN BIKING IS A POPULAR ACTIVITY ON MOUNT HOOD'S LAUREL HILL—A FAR DIFFERENT TRIP FROM WHEN OREGON TRAIL IMMIGRANTS ROPED THEIR WAGONS DOWN THIS SLOPE. RIGHT: THE ROCKY BUTTE AREA OF NORTHEAST PORTLAND OFFERS MOUNTAIN BIKE PATHS. *PHOTOS BY STEVE TERRILL*

Residents have access to some of the most challenging and varied hiking and climbing terrain in the world.

CLACKAMAS COUNTY
HIKING TRAILS
OFFER HIKERS AND
BACKPACKERS
OUTSTANDING VIEWS OF
MOUNT HOOD. *PHOTO
BY LARRY GEDDIS*

WINDSURFERS FROM
AROUND THE WORLD
CONVERGE ON HOOD
RIVER TO ENJOY NEAR-
PERFECT WINDSURFING
CONDITIONS, AN EASY
DRIVE FROM PORTLAND.
PHOTO BY LARRY GEDDIS

PADDLE BOATS AT
CLEAWOX LAKE IN J.M.
HONEYMAN STATE PARK
ON THE SOUTH CENTRAL
OREGON COAST. *PHOTO
BY STEVE TERRILL*

GREAT FISHING AND
BOATING CAN BE FOUND
ON LAKES AND RIVERS
THROUGHOUT THE
STATE. HERE, "BANKIES"
CAST A LINE AT BENSON
STATE PARK, IN THE
COLUMBIA RIVER
GORGE. *PHOTO BY
STEVE TERRILL*

The snowfields of Mount Hood cast a magic spell on skiers and snowboarders during all four seasons.

BUILT OF NATIVE STONE AND LOGS, HISTORIC TIMBERLINE LODGE HAS OFFERED LODGING AND MEALS TO MOUNT HOOD SKIERS AND VISITORS FOR MORE THAN SIXTY YEARS. *PHOTO BY LARRY GEDDIS*

SILHOUETTED AGAINST AN EARLY EVENING SKY, FOUR RIDERS ENJOY THE SPECTACULAR SCENERY TO BE FOUND IN THE COLUMBIA GORGE. *PHOTO BY STEVE TERRILL*

OPPOSITE PAGE: YELLOW AND RED MONKEY FLOWERS BLOOM ALONG MCGEE CREEK, WITH MOUNT HOOD IN THE BACKGROUND. *PHOTO BY LARRY GEDDIS*

THANKS TO AN ACTIVE
RESTORATION PROGRAM
ON THE COLUMBIA
SLOUGH, HUNDREDS OF
SPECIES OF BIRDS AND
ANIMALS, FROM WILD
DUCKS AND GEESE
TO BALD EAGLES,
PEREGRINE FALCONS,
WILLOW FLYCATCHERS,
MINKS, RIVER OTTERS,
BEAVERS, COYOTES, AND
WESTERN POND AND
PAINTED TURTLES ARE
ATTRACTED TO THIS CITY
TREASURE. THE SLOUGH
IS ALSO A GREENWAY
AND RECREATIONAL
CORRIDOR FOR PEOPLE.
PHOTO BY STEVE TERRILL

"With the heavy investment we make toward the training of our workforce, Purdy's commitment to the Portland area is a strong one. As a company that understands the importance of team effort, athletic-related pursuits like youth sports, Pee Wee, and Little League baseball are natural civic causes for the Purdy Company to support. We also feel that we can frequently be counted on to be among those who donate products for local construction-related causes as well."

David E. Howard, Jr.
Vice President of Marketing
Purdy Corporation

SAILBOATS AT PORTLAND YACHT CLUB EMERGE FROM AN EARLY MORNING FOG LIKE SOME MYSTICAL GHOST FLEET. *PHOTO BY STEVE TERRILL*

RIGHT AND
OPPOSITE PAGE: FROM
COMPETITIVE LEAGUE
PLAY TO A QUICK
PICK-UP GAME, SOCCER
FLOURISHES IN
PORTLAND! AND
FERNHILL PARK, ABLAZE
WITH AUTUMN COLORS,
IS THE PERFECT PLACE
FOR FRIENDS AND
FAMILY TO GATHER FOR
THE DAY TO CHEER
THEIR FAVORITE TEAM.
*PHOTOS BY
STEVE TERRILL*

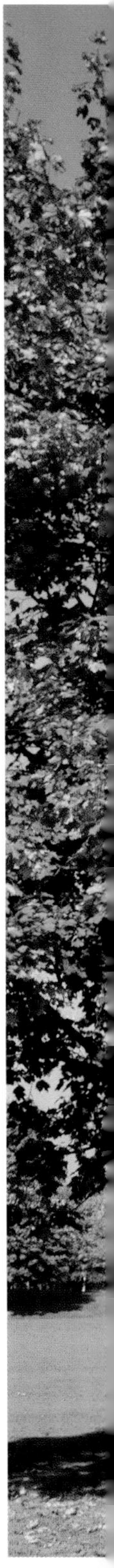

THERE IS A LOT OF
SOFTBALL IN PORTLAND!
THROUGH THE
PORTLAND METRO
SOFTBALL ASSOCIATION,
10,000 PEOPLE PLAY
SUMMER AND FALL
SOFTBALL ON 700
TEAMS. CELEBRATING
ITS 67TH YEAR IN 2002,
THE ASSOCIATION
HOSTED THE MEN'S
SLOWPITCH "B"
WESTERN NATIONALS
IN 2001. *PHOTO BY
STEVE TERRILL*

CENTERPIECE OF THE
MORE THAN 100
PORTLAND PARKS AND
RECREATION SOFTBALL
FIELDS ACROSS THE
CITY, THE WILLIAM V.
OWENS SOFTBALL
COMPLEX INCLUDES FIVE
FIELDS WITH TWO MORE
ADJACENT. THE CITY
LEAGUE OPERATES IN
CONJUNCTION WITH
PORTLAND METRO
SOFTBALL ASSOCIATION,
AND INCLUDES THE
JUNIOR OLYMPICS GIRLS
FAST PITCH YOUTH
PROGRAM. THE 2001
SOFTBALL LITTLE
LEAGUE WORLD SERIES
JAMBOREE WAS ALSO
HELD HERE. *PHOTO BY
STEVE TERRILL*

PORTLAND'S TEMPERATE YEAR-ROUND CLIMATE AND EASY ACCESSIBILITY TO VARIED TERRAIN, FROM THE MOUNTAINS, TO THE BEACH, TO THE DESERT, ARE A GOLFER'S DREAM COME TRUE. THE CITY HOSTED FOUR USGA EVENTS IN 2000 AT VARIOUS COURSES. PETER JACOBSON'S ANNUAL FRED MEYER CHALLENGE IS HOSTED AT THE RESERVE VINEYARDS GOLF CLUB. *PHOTO BY STEVE TERRILL*

SOME FIFTY-EIGHT PUBLIC AND TWELVE PRIVATE GOLF COURSES IN THE PORTLAND AREA OFFER GOLFERS NUMEROUS CHOICES, FROM EXECUTIVE TO PROFESSIONAL-LEVEL PLAY. A NUMBER OF GOLF RESORTS ARE WITHIN AN EASY DRIVE. *PHOTO BY STEVE TERRILL*

CHAPTER FOUR

BY GEORGE TAYLOR

The Arts

PORTLAND OPERA'S SCHEDULE INCLUDES PERFORMANCES SUCH AS *COSI FAN TUTTE*, *LA TRAVIATA*, *THE PEARL FISHERS*, *THE CONSUL*, AND *CANDIDE*, BUT IN ADDITION TO FINE PROFESSIONAL OPERA, THE EDUCATION AND OUTREACH DEPARTMENT REACHES OVER 80,000 PEOPLE YEARLY THROUGH PROGRAMS LIKE THE GEARY FOUNDATION STUDENT DRESS REHEARSAL, PREVIEW PRESENTATIONS, PROGRAMS FOR THE SCHOOLS, THE INTERNATIONAL VOCAL ARTS INSTITUTE, AND PORTLAND OPERA WORKS! *PHOTO BY DUANE MORRIS/ COURTESY OF THE PORTLAND OPERA*

On a Friday night in late September, my wife, Edie, and I attended the opening of *The Devils*, a modern dramatization of Dostoevski's novel. Saturday, we dropped in at the Portland Art Museum to check out the recent $20 million expansion. That night, it was the opera *Carmen*. On Sunday, pianist Nikolai Lugansky played Beethoven; on Monday, the Portland Baroque Orchestra played Bach; on Tuesday, the Takacs String Quartet played Janacek.

Wednesday, we caught a production of *Beauty Queen of Leenane*. Thursday was First Thursday, when the galleries open their new shows and thousands of Portlanders turn it into a street festival. Just had time for a quick in-and-out at four galleries before curtain for *Life Is a Dream*. We ended the week appropriately at a Nerve Endings Concert by the Oregon Symphony.

On Saturday, realizing that we'd barely scratched the surface, we collapsed.

Portland is a city working hard to find room for all the art happening here, and the result—for arts lovers, at least—can seem like one of those renaissance banquets you read about. Try as you might, you can't take in everything.

George Thorn, a Portland-based arts consultant who works with organizations and communities nationwide, calls Portland "as diverse a community for the arts as you'll find anywhere. The opportunity to see things is very high…You go out of town, you fall behind." The quality, he notes, largely equals that in other regions. But where Portland has an edge—reflecting its progressive approach toward city life, perhaps—is in its openness to new works and new forms.

The classics are not ignored, of course. Not in Shakespeare- and Bach-loving Portland. The Oregon Symphony, for instance, presents two classical series each season, as well as a variety of pops and family concerts. But it has also created a new form—the "dramatic concert." Called Nerve Endings, and featuring themes like Sigmund Freud and the Dreams of Gustav Mahler, the concerts use music, narration, and imagination to connect audiences with the art and their own lives.

The Portland Youth Philharmonic has provided many of the musicians to the Oregon Symphony, as well as to orchestras across the country, from the New York Philharmonic, to the Boston Symphony, the National Symphony, and the Julliard and American String Quartets. The Portland Youth Philharmonic discovers and develops latent talent among the children of Portland, giving them the opportunity to perform in public symphonies and popular concerts.

OPPOSITE PAGE: THE OLDEST PIECE OF PUBLIC ART IN PORTLAND, THE SKIDMORE FOUNTAIN IS IN ANKENY PLAZA IN PORTLAND'S OLD TOWN. INSCRIBED "GOOD CITIZENS ARE THE RICHES OF A CITY," THE FOUNTAIN WAS GIVEN AS A GIFT TO THE CITY IN 1888 BY STEPHEN SKIDMORE, SO PEOPLE AND ANIMALS COULD BOTH SLAKE THEIR THIRSTS FROM IT. *PHOTO BY LARRY GEDDIS*

Portland has an edge in its openness to new works and new forms.

Chamber Music Northwest produces a five-week summer festival and a series of winter concerts, where audiences regularly encounter music from the seventeenth century through the twenty-first, performed by some of the world's finest musicians. Other ensembles, notably Third Angle and Fear No Music, are known for thrilling performances of new music. Old music is the specialty of Portland Baroque Orchestra, which performs with fresh brilliance on period instruments.

Portland Opera does an outstanding job with masterworks of the Italian, French, and German repertoire. Season highlights, however, are often productions of rarely-seen works, such as a recent mounting of *The Love for Three Oranges*.

Oregon Ballet Theatre also produces its share of beloved classics, including an annual *Nutcracker* that's a must-see for thousands of families. But the company is equally noted for edgy new works, some decidedly R-rated. Among the hottest tickets in town is anything by White Bird Dance, which presents such exciting modern dance companies as Bill T. Jones and Alvin Ailey.

The theater scene is just as varied. Portland Center Stage (PCS), the city's largest company, opened a dozen years ago as an extension of the Oregon Shakespeare Festival. Today, as an independent theater, PCS produces a season that ranges from contemporary and newly commissioned plays to Shakespeare and other classics.

Nearby in Portland's downtown arts district, Artists Repertory Theatre concentrates on daring productions of newer works and insightful stagings of older ones. Tygres Heart limits itself to a single playwright, but that playwright is William Shakespeare, still arguably the theater's most modern writer.

The East Side might well be called Portland's off-Broadway district. Here, Imago creates what some consider the most unexpected theater in the city. Do Jump! Extremely Physical Theatre stretches the meanings of both dance and theater.

One of the most distinctive approaches is taken by Profile Theatre Project. The company focuses on a single playwright each season, giving audiences a chance to explore the work of such icons of the theater as Arthur Miller in rare depth.

The East Side is also home to the Hispanic-themed Miracle Theatre Group; Musical Theatre Company; Triangle Productions, whose plays often have a gay orientation; Stark Raving Theatre; and more others than you'd think could fit into a city this size.

Most companies produce at least one family-friendly production a season, and many have extensive educational programs. The Northwest Children's Theater and Oregon Children's Theatre are located in Portland, as well. Another company, Tears of Joy, is nationally known for innovative puppetry that amazes children and adults alike.

Despite these riches, many feel that Portland's real strength lies in the visual arts. The most prominent manifestation, of course, is the Portland Art Museum, which has become one of Portland's most popular places to see art–and to be seen.

But the arts story also includes a vibrant gallery scene that extends from the surging Pearl District, to the business core, to emerging gallery rows like Alberta Street in Northeast Portland. And it includes organizations like the Portland Institute for Contemporary Art. "PICA," says Eloise Damrosch, public art director of the Regional Arts and Culture Council, "has really made a difference. All the dot-com types go straight to PICA to find out what's hip."

One reason for the richness is the solid educational base provided by the Portland institutions: the Northwest College of Art and the Oregon College of Art and Craft. Then, too, art prices in Portland are lower than in many other cities. Art lovers here can actually afford to buy.

Of course, Portlanders already own an incredibly valuable art collection. "You can't walk very far without bumping into public art," Damrosch says. "People come here and say, 'I can't believe it, there's art everywhere." Portland's percent-for-the-arts program, which mandates that a percentage of major construction budgets be dedicated for public art, was one of the nation's first and is still one of the most-imitated. Through the program, artists were included as part of the design team for Portland's West Side light rail system. "It's amazing how much of an impact your art dollars can have if artists are part of the development process," says Damrosch. The impact can be seen in every station along the line, in the seamless, natural integration of art and infrastructure.

That kind of urban environment is at the core of City Commissioner Charlie Hales's vision for Portland. Hales

recently added arts and culture to a portfolio that also includes planning/development, and transportation, making it somewhat easier to achieve the goal of weaving art into key city infrastructure. "Arts are the tapestry of a city," Hales says. "They add value to our daily lives."

LEFT AND FAR LEFT: FOUNDED IN 1988, THE OREGON CHILDREN'S THEATRE (OCT) PRODUCES THREE PLAYS A YEAR BASED ON CLASSIC CHILDREN'S BOOKS AND DESIGNED TO TIE IN WITH SCHOOL LITERATURE PROGRAMS. A POPULAR FIELD TRIP DESTINATION, THE OCT CELEBRATED ITS ONE-MILLIONTH PATRON IN 2000, AND BOASTS AUDIENCES IN EXCESS OF 100,000 YEARLY. POPULAR WITH FAMILIES, OCT PRODUCTIONS ARE FUNDED BY TICKET SALES AND DONATIONS, AND FEATURE PROFESSIONAL ACTORS, WITH CHILDREN CAST IN AGE-APPROPRIATE ROLES. *PHOTO BY DUANE MORRIS/ COURTESY OF OREGON CHILDREN'S THEATRE* BOTTOM: ARTISTS REPERTORY THEATRE PRODUCTIONS EXPLORE THE STRENGTH, FRAILTY, AND DIVERSITY OF THE HUMAN CONDITION THROUGH REGIONAL PREMIERS, COMMUNITY WORKS, AND SELECTED CLASSICS APPROPRIATE TO CONTEMPORARY ISSUES. *PHOTO BY OWEN CAREY/COURTESY OF ARTISTS REPERTORY THEATRE*

"FIRST THURSDAY" MONTHLY OFFICIAL GALLERY OPENINGS DOWNTOWN AND IN THE PEARL DISTRICT ARE A POPULAR PORTLAND TRADITION. GALLERY-GOERS TRAVEL FROM ONE TO THE NEXT, VISITING WITH FRIENDS AND VIEWING EXCITING NEW WORKS. *PHOTO BY STEVE TERRILL*

THE HIGHLY-ACCLAIMED MUSIC DEPARTMENT OF MT. HOOD COMMUNITY COLLEGE ATTRACTS TOP MUSIC STUDENTS FROM THROUGHOUT THE NORTHWEST ON A COMPETITIVE BASIS. ITS AWARD-WINNING VOCAL AND INSTRUMENTAL ENSEMBLES INCLUDE VOCAL JAZZ AND STRING ENSEMBLES, JAZZ AND SYMPHONY BANDS, AND SYMPHONIC AND CHAMBER CHOIRS. *PHOTO BY JANET BRAYSON/COURTESY OF MT. HOOD COMMUNITY COLLEGE*

*Portland is a city working hard
to find room for all the art happening here*

Leaders in business, government, and the arts are busily exploring a variety of innovative public-private partnerships to give the arts and artists the support they need. And Thorn points to recent fund-raising successes as a hint that Portland may be ready for a new level of philanthropy. "Giving substantial money and being recognized for it is no longer seen as ostentatious." ■

FAR LEFT: PERFORMANCES OF ALL KINDS ARE REGULARLY OFFERED BY UNIVERSITIES AND COLLEGES ACROSS THE CITY AT LITTLE OR NO COST. THIS FLAUTIST IS A STUDENT IN THE WARNER PACIFIC COLLEGE WIND ENSEMBLE COURSE. *PHOTO BY DEREK BRADFORD/COURTESY OF WARNER PACIFIC COLLEGE*

LEFT: WITH THE PORTLAND SKYLINE AND THE WEST HILLS AS A BACKDROP, ARTIST TOM OTTERNESS CREATED THESE WHIMSICAL BRONZE ANIMALS FOR THE 9TH FLOOR OPEN TERRACE OF THE MARK HATFIELD FEDERAL COURTHOUSE. *PHOTO BY LARRY GEDDIS*

BOTTOM: EACH JULY, BUSINESS-SPONSORED TEAMS CREATE WHIMSICAL SAND SCULPTURES IN DOWNTOWN PORTLAND'S PIONEER COURTHOUSE SQUARE. YOSHIDA'S SAND IN THE CITY BENEFITS THE KIDS ON THE BLOCK AWARENESS PROGRAM. ENTITLED *EVERY KID DESERVES THE BEST*, THESE CHESS PIECES WERE CREATED BY THE OHSU-DOERNBECHER CHILDREN'S HOSPITAL TEAM. *PHOTO BY LARRY GEDDIS*

*Many feel that Portland's real strength
lies in the visual arts*

THE OLDEST FINE ARTS
MUSEUM IN THE
NORTHWEST, THE
PORTLAND ART MUSEUM
REGULARLY ATTRACTS
WORLD-CLASS EXHIBITS.
RANKED AS ONE OF THE
TWENTY-FIVE LARGEST
MUSEUMS IN NORTH
AMERICA, ITS PERMA-
NENT COLLECTION
INCLUDES MORE THAN
32,000 WORKS OF ART
FROM AROUND THE
WORLD, IN A 240,000-
SQUARE-FOOT CAMPUS.
PHOTO BY STEVE TERRILL

*PHOTO BY EDIS JURCYS/
COURTESY OF PORTLAND
ART MUSEUM*

THIS PAGE AND OPPOSITE PAGE BOTTOM: THE NEWLY-RENOVATED HOFFMAN WING, LOCATED IN THE PORTLAND ART MUSEUM COMPLEX, HOUSES ONE OF THE THREE MOST IMPORTANT COLLECTIONS OF NATIVE AMERICAN ART IN THE COUNTRY, AND INCLUDES THE CONFEDERATED TRIBES OF THE GRAND RONDE CENTER FOR NATIVE AMERICAN ART, AS WELL AS THE SCHNITZER CENTER FOR NORTHWEST ART. IN ADDITION TO ITS PERMANENT COLLECTION, THE MUSEUM DEDICATES 9,000 SQUARE FEET EXCLUSIVELY TO SPECIAL TRAVELING EXHIBITIONS, WITH ONE OR TWO GENERALLY AVAILABLE FOR VIEWING. *TOP PHOTOS BY EDIS JURCYS/COURTESY OF PORTLAND ART MUSEUM, BOTTOM PHOTO BY YALCIN ERHAN/ COURTESY OF PORTLAND ART MUSEUM*

CITY-OWNED, THE PORTLAND CENTER FOR PERFORMING ARTS INCLUDES THE KELLER AUDITORIUM, FORMERLY THE CIVIC AUDITORIUM, WITH SEATING FOR 2,992. THE CENTER'S MAIN COMPLEX, ON SOUTHEAST BROADWAY IN THE CULTURAL DISTRICT, INCLUDES THE ARLENE SCHNITZER CONCERT HALL, THE SECOND LARGEST FACILITY, WHICH SEATS 2,776; THE NEWMARK THEATRE; THE DOLORES WINNINGSTAD THEATRE; AND BRUNISH HALL, A 3,500-SQUARE-FOOT MULTI-PURPOSE FACILITY. MORE THAN ONE MILLION VIEW THE 1,000-PLUS EVENTS HELD IN THE CENTER EACH YEAR.

PHOTO BY LARRY GEDDIS

"Francis Bacon said that the role of the artist was to 'deepen the mystery.' Our role, in health care, is to work towards giving patients a longer, healthier life–to renew them both physically and emotionally when possible. We believe that the greatest thing we can do, in this profession, is to help patients more fully enjoy the beauty and mystery that is life, and the world we live in."

Joel Preston Smith
Public Affairs Officer
Portland Veterans Affairs Medical Center

"Arts are the tapestry of a city, . . .
they add value to our daily lives."

TOP: KNOWN FOR ITS UNIQUE COMMITMENT TO SHOWCASING WHAT IS INVENTIVE IN BALLET TODAY AND TO PROVIDING OPPORTUNITIES FOR EMERGING AMERICAN CHOREOGRAPHERS, THE OREGON BALLET THEATRE (OBT) IS A CLASSICALLY-BASED PORTLAND PROFESSIONAL BALLET COMPANY. EACH YEAR, OBT PRODUCES TWO EVENTS NOT TO BE SEEN ANYWHERE ELSE IN THE COUNTRY, AND THE SEASON FINALE IS THE AMERICAN CHOREOGRAPHERS SHOWCASE. *PHOTO COURTESY OF OREGON BALLET THEATRE, © RAFAEL ASTORGA*

BOTTOM: DO JUMP! EXTREMELY PHYSICAL THEATRE COMPANY HAS CAPTURED AUDIENCE IMAGINATION FOR MORE THAN TWO DECADES WITH ITS UNIQUE COMBINATION OF HUMOR, MUSIC, DANCE, THEATER, AND ACROBATICS. *PHOTO BY JOHN KLICKER/ COURTESY OF DO JUMP!*

OPPOSITE PAGE: THE NATIONALLY-ACCLAIMED OREGON SYMPHONY, UNDER THE DIRECTION OF MUSIC DIRECTOR AND COMPOSER JAMES DEPRIEST, HAS BECOME ONE OF THE FINEST MAJOR ORCHESTRAS IN THE NATION, WITH ANNUAL AUDIENCES OF MORE THAN 320,000. *PHOTO BY STEVE TERRILL*

CHAPTER FIVE

BY RUSSELL NELSON

Education

There's an old pioneer story that settlers headed west would come to a fork in the trail somewhere near the Rockies. Beside the right fork was a sign that said "To Oregon." By the left fork was a large pile of rocks glittering with iron pyrite.

According to the story, those who could read came to Oregon.

That same pioneering spirit and regard for learning are still at work in Portland's public schools, colleges, and universities.

Portland Public Schools (PPS) is an ethnically and racially diverse district, serving 55,000 students in 100 schools and fifty special-needs sites. PPS diversifies educational programs among its schools, particularly at the high school level, and one fourth of the district's students choose schools outside their neighborhoods in order to find programs that best meet their goals.

Each of the district's high schools has its own academic identity. Jefferson High School offers performing arts programs, while Cleveland High focuses on business, finance, and marketing. Benson Polytechnic offers programs in engineering and technology plus vocational skills, while Marshall features a manufacturing program linked to the high-tech industry. Grant offers its Institute for Science and Math, while Wilson stresses college preparation. Lincoln features international studies and, with Cleveland, offers an International Baccalaureate Program.

There are other alternatives, as well. At Metropolitan Learning Center students design their own educational programs. Vocational Village uses small, informal classes to teach trades and vocations. The Portland Night School offers classes for students unable to attend traditional high school classes during the day.

Ninety percent of Portland students attend public schools rather than private schools, the highest percentage of any major urban district in the country. Not that private schools are lacking. There are many quality private schools in the area offering smaller class sizes, individual attention, and high academic standards.

Stretching from Portland to the Coast Range, Portland Community College (PCC) is a pioneer in taking the classroom to the community. Each year nearly 97,000 students, almost one in ten district residents, attend classes at PCC, making it the largest institution of higher learning in Oregon. Enrollment has grown five percent annually for the past four years.

Mt. Hood Community College in Gresham to the east, and Clackamas Community College in Oregon City to the south, provide excellent options as well, with specialized programs and strong community support.

Portland Public Schools is an ethnically and racially diverse district, serving 55,000 students.

Many students choose a community college for the first two years, and then transfer to participating colleges and universities in Oregon without losing credits. Other students will complete their education with an Associate Degree or other certificate chosen from the dozens of disciplines available through the community college programs. Thousands of other students attend community colleges to further their career, complete high school, learn basic skills, or pursue personal interests.

PCC campuses include the Cascade Campus serving north Portland, the Washington County Rock Creek Campus west of Portland, and the Sylvania Campus in suburban southwest Portland. All three campuses offer complete academic programs, educational facilities, and support services.

Specialized programs are offered through the PCC Southeast Center and the three Workforce Training Centers (WTC). The Southeast Center offers evening and weekend classes for working adults. Programs include General Education Development (GED), English as a Second Language (ESL), adult basic education, and vocational training. College transfer classes are also given.

The Portland Metropolitan WTC in Northeast Portland offers classes including professional development, welfare-to-work programs, and the Dislocated Workers Project. The Central Portland WTC provides courses for business people and professionals in the downtown area. The Washington County WTC offers model public-private programs in cooperation with Portland's fast-growing high-tech industry.

Oregon Health & Science University (OHSU) is more than an institution of higher learning. While OHSU offers medical, dental, and nursing degrees, it also promotes clinical research and provides superior patient care. These services along with educational and outreach programs work together to support OHSU's mission to improve the overall quality of human health through teaching and application.

Located downtown along the South Park Blocks, Portland State University (PSU) is the only urban university in the Oregon State University System and has grown to become the largest university in the state.

PSU offers more than 100 undergraduate and graduate degrees. Schools and colleges within the university include Liberal Arts and Sciences, Urban and Public Affairs, Education, Social Work, Business Administration, Engineering and Applied Science, and Fine and Performing Arts. Students also are required to do community projects where they apply classroom theory to real world problems.

RIGHT: RECESS IS GREAT! THESE SMILING STUDENTS ARE TAKING A STUDY BREAK AT AN ELEMENTARY SCHOOL IN EAST MULTNOMAH COUNTY'S CENTENNIAL DISTRICT. FAR RIGHT: STUDENTS ARE INTRODUCED AT A YOUNG AGE TO TECHNOLOGY THROUGH COMPUTER LABS IN PORTLAND-AREA ELEMENTARY SCHOOLS. *PHOTOS BY LARRY GEDDIS*

While some programs move students from the university to the real world, others bring students from the real world to the university. The School of Extended Studies serves students who have full-time jobs and commitments, and want to continue their education. Instruction is offered on- and off-campus, through on-line courses, and in the workplace.

Lewis & Clark College is located a few miles south of downtown Portland. A nationally-ranked private college, Lewis & Clark offers academic programs intended for the "academic elite, not the economic elite." The college confers undergraduate and graduate degrees, and offers three dozen major and minor courses of study. Lewis & Clark's Northwestern School of Law is well-known, particularly in areas such as environmental law and intellectual property law.

Reed College is another nationally ranked private college located in Portland. With approximately 1,350 students and a student to faculty ratio near 10:1, Reed represents a closely knit intellectual community dedicated to academic excellence. The College offers courses in five divisions: Arts; Literature and Languages; History and Social Sciences; Math and Natural Sciences; and Philosophy, Psychology, and Religion. Through Reed's international studies exchange program, students can attend participating universities in a dozen foreign countries.

The University of Portland, located in the north section of the city, is a Catholic school offering a liberal arts education "devoted to the heart and spirit as much as the mind." The University enrolls approximately 2,600 students, and offers both undergraduate and graduate degree programs. Students choose from fifty majors in the schools of Arts and Science, Business Administration, Education, Engineering, and Nursing. There are seventeen graduate degree programs in nine academic areas.

Concordia University is a liberal arts school affiliated with the Lutheran Church. Located near downtown Portland, Concordia University is part of the Concordia University System, a consortium of ten U.S. Christian colleges and universities. The 1,000 plus students who attend Concordia pursue studies including Psychology, Biology, Theology, Health and Fitness Management, Humanities, and Education. Concordia University students enjoy a small campus environment in a major urban setting.

Warner Pacific College is a liberal arts school operated under the auspices of the Church of God. The college offers instructional programs in the departments of Business, Education, Health and Human Kinetics, Humanities, Music, Religion and Christian Ministries, Science and Math, and Social Science. Degrees offered at Warner Pacific include Associate of Arts or Science, Bachelor of Arts or Science, and Master of Religion.

LEFT: SCHOOL CHILDREN ENJOY AN OUTING IN DOWNTOWN PORTLAND'S PIONEER COURTHOUSE SQUARE— A GREAT PLACE TO SIT, TALK, AND ENJOY THE AFTERNOON SUN. *PHOTO BY LARRY GEDDIS*
FAR LEFT: LEARNING GOES ON BOTH INSIDE AND OUTSIDE THE CLASSROOM IN THE PORTLAND PUBLIC SCHOOLS. ELEMENTARY STUDENTS TAKE THE HANDS-ON APPROACH TO STUDYING AQUATIC LIFE AT FAIRVIEW CREEK WETLANDS. *PHOTO BY LARRY GEDDIS*

Marylhurst University near Lake Oswego is an innovative school devoted to making "post-secondary education accessible to self-directed students of any age." Marylhurst offers fourteen undergraduate and five graduate degrees in Management, Communications, Science, Social Sciences, Human Studies, Music, Art, and other disciplines. Many classes and some degrees are offered through the Internet.

Many educational opportunities abound just beyond the metropolitan area. These include colleges and universities such as the University of Oregon, Oregon State University, George Fox University, Willamette University, Linfield College, and Pacific University.

Much has changed since those literate pioneers settled along the Willamette River, but the respect for education they instilled remains as strong today as their pioneering spirit was a century and a half ago. ■

"SRG is a respected leader in the design and planning of facilities for both the public and private sector. We strive for imaginative, insightful, and refreshing designs that reveal the fundamental character of each project. More than 20 college campuses in Oregon, California, Washington, and Idaho and have selected SRG to meet their diverse project needs, including instructional and academic use, libraries, computer science, museums, marine research, veterinary medicine, and biomedical research."

Jon Schleuning, FAIA
Design Principal
SRG Partnership, PC

A pioneering spirit and regard for learning are still at work in Portland's schools, colleges, and universities.

LEWIS & CLARK COLLEGE, THE LARGEST INDEPENDENT COLLEGE IN OREGON, EMPHASIZES AN INFORMED RESPECT FOR THE NATURAL ENVIRONMENT AND ACTIVE INQUIRY BY FACULTY AND STUDENTS. THE SCHOOL INCLUDES ITS COLLEGE OF ARTS AND SCIENCES, GRADUATE SCHOOL OF PROFESSIONAL STUDIES, NORTHWESTERN SCHOOL OF LAW, AND INSTITUTE FOR THE STUDY OF AMERICAN LANGUAGE AND CULTURE. *PHOTO COURTESY OF LEWIS & CLARK COLLEGE*

Some programs move students from the university to the real world.

BEAUTIFULLY SITUATED AROUND THE TREE-LINED SOUTH PARK BLOCKS IN DOWNTOWN PORTLAND, PORTLAND STATE UNIVERSITY SERVES MORE STUDENTS, AND CONFERS MORE GRADUATE DEGREES ANNUALLY THAN ANY OTHER OREGON UNIVERSITY. *PHOTO BY STEVE DIPAOLA/ COURTESY OF PORTLAND STATE UNIVERSITY*

LOCATED IN THE DOWNTOWN HEART OF OREGON'S ECONOMIC AND CULTURAL ACTIVITY, PORTLAND STATE UNIVERSITY PROVIDES THE IDEAL ENVIRONMENT FOR STUDENTS AND FACULTY TO APPLY SCHOLARLY THEORY TO REAL-WORLD BUSINESS AND COMMUNITY ISSUES. THE UNIVERSITY OFFERS MORE THAN 100 UNDERGRADUATE, MASTER'S AND DOCTORAL DEGREES, AS WELL AS GRADUATE CERTIFICATES AND CONTINUING EDUCATION PROGRAMS. *PHOTO BY GERRY KANO/COURTESY OF PORTLAND STATE UNIVERSITY*

Others bring students from the real world to the university.

REED COLLEGE STUDENTS RECEIVE A DISPROPORTIONATE NUMBER OF NATIONAL SCIENCE FOUNDATION GRADUATE FELLOWSHIPS, GIVEN THE SCHOOL'S SMALL STUDENT BODY, REAFFIRMING ITS HISTORIC STRENGTH IN THE SCIENCES. REED HAS PRODUCED THIRTY RHODES SCHOLARS, AND THIRTEEN ALUMNI HAVE BEEN ELECTED INTO THE NATIONAL ACADEMY OF SCIENCES. *PHOTO BY STEVE WANKE/COURTESY OF REED COLLEGE*

TERMED "THE MOST INTELLECTUAL COLLEGE IN THE COUNTRY" BY A FORMER EDUCATION EDITOR OF THE *NEW YORK TIMES*, REED COLLEGE'S ENTERING FRESHMEN AVERAGE A 3.7 HIGH SCHOOL GPA. EIGHTY-TWO PERCENT RANKED IN THE TOP FIFTH OF THEIR HIGH SCHOOL CLASSES, AND EIGHTY-TWO PERCENT WERE VALEDICTORIANS. *PHOTO BY STEVE WANKE/COURTESY OF REED COLLEGE*

THE HOSPITALS AND
CLINICS OF OREGON
HEALTH & SCIENCE
UNIVERSITY (OHSU)
ARE THE STATE'S
MAIN SOURCES FOR
CLINICAL TRAINING OF
TOMORROW'S HEALTH
PROFESSIONALS, AND
FOR CLINICAL
RESEARCH. MANY OF ITS
INNOVATIVE CLINICAL
CARE AND DIAGNOSTIC
SERVICES ARE NOT
AVAILABLE ANYWHERE
ELSE IN THE STATE OR
REGION. OHSU HOSPITAL
PROVIDES THE MOST
COMPREHENSIVE
HEALTH-CARE SERVICES
IN OREGON—FROM
ROUTINE SERVICES
TO COMPLEX AND
REVOLUTIONARY
SPECIALTY TREATMENTS.
PHOTO BY LARRY GEDDIS

TOP LEFT: A PIONEER OF INNOVATIVE POST-SECONDARY EDUCATION, MARYLHURST UNIVERSITY OFFERS COURSE WORK LEADING TO BACHELOR AND MASTER'S DEGREES FOR SELF-DIRECTED STUDENTS. WITH ITS CATHOLIC AND LIBERAL ARTS HERITAGE, THE SCHOOL PROMOTES RESPONSIBLE PARTICIPATION IN A RAPIDLY CHANGING WORLD. *PHOTO BY DAVE BRUNKOW/COURTESY OF MARYLHURST UNIVERSITY*

TOP RIGHT: THE UNIVERSITY OF PORTLAND (UP), A CATHOLIC LIBERAL ARTS UNIVERSITY, IS "DEVOTED TO THE HEART AND SPIRIT AS MUCH AS THE MIND." ENROLLING SOME 2,600 STUDENTS, UP OFFERS UNDERGRADUATE DEGREES IN FIFTY MAJOR AREAS OF STUDY, AND SEVENTEEN GRADUATE DEGREE PROGRAMS.

BOTTOM: UNIVERSITY OF PORTLAND FANS SHOW THEIR APPROVAL AT A RECENT SPORTS EVENT. OPEN TO THE PUBLIC, SPORTS ACTIVITIES AT AREA COLLEGES ARE WELL-ATTENDED. *PHOTOS COURTESY OF UNIVERSITY OF PORTLAND*

CHAPTER SIX

BY DICK MONTGOMERY

Transportation

With its population burgeoning to 12,000 souls, rainy and sometimes-flooded early Portland needed to get its citizens "out of the mud."

Colorful railroad builder and early overland stagecoach operator Ben Holladay was awarded a franchise in 1872 to operate the Portland Street Railway Co. Holladay's horse-cars followed tracks along the riverbank on First Avenue for two miles through the retail business district and into the residential neighborhood. Horse-cars took city residents out of the mud, to work, and back home again. They had few other places to go.

Today, sleek Eastside and Westside light rail coaches still run along First Avenue as they serpentine to Portland suburbs: east 15 miles to Gresham; and west 18 miles to Beaverton and Hillsboro, and soon, into North Portland.

Light rail serves Portland International Airport (PDX), a project hailed nationally as the first-of-its-kind to cost-share with the private sector to fund a public light rail line.

Tri-Met's (Tri-County Metropolitan Transportation District of Oregon) well-patronized MAX light rail lines augment more than 100 city bus lines that criss-cross Portland. The system was recognized as America's best large-transit agency by the American Public Transit Association in 1989. Tri-Met carried more than 272,200 daily riders during 2000.

Included among riders are those aboard a vintage streetcar that runs from Portland's Old Town to Lloyd Center. The new Portland Street Car, Inc., runs from the Good Samaritan Hospital area in Northwest Portland to Portland State University in the Southwest section of the city.

In 1978, Portland gained national attention when it built a Transit Mall in the heart of its downtown area. This innovation, spearheaded by Mayor Neil Goldschmidt, later Secretary of Transportation under President Jimmy Carter, and then Governor of Oregon, is credited with making Portland's downtown one of the most vibrant, attractive, and economically successful in the U.S.

Also two decades ago, Portland gained fame and set a nationwide example when it replaced a six-lane freeway along the Willamette River with Tom McCall Waterfront Park.

Adding to Portland's transportation options is an efficient bus-rail transportation center complex in Northwest Portland. Here, at the foot of the Broadway Bridge, historic Union Station offers nationwide AmTrak services. Nearby, the contemporary Greyhound Bus Terminal operates from 5 A.M. to 1 A.M., seven days a week, offering regional bus schedules.

The rivers that ring Portland, encompassing 52 miles on the Willamette and the Columbia, are enjoyed by well over 100,000 registered boaters plus a vast flotilla of rowboats,

Portland's downtown is one of the most vibrant, attractive, and economically successful in the U.S.

RIGHT: EVERY DAY AT NOON, PORTLANDERS CAN BE FOUND WALKING OR JOGGING ALONG THE WEST SEA WALL OF TOM MCCALL WATERFRONT PARK DOWNTOWN. NATURE-LOVING PORTLANDERS TORE DOWN AND RELOCATED A FREEWAY TO BUILD THE PARK ALONG THE RIVER. *PHOTO BY LARRY GEDDIS*

BOTTOM: PORTLAND IS ONE OF THE MOST BIKE-FRIENDLY CITIES IN THE NATION. ITS NEIGHBORHOODS ARE CONNECTED BY 200 MILES OF BIKEWAYS ACROSS THE CITY. *PHOTO BY STEVE TERRILL*

canoes, and personal watercraft. Nearly a dozen cruise ships offer Portlanders and visitors a variety of scenic experiences on the water, and plans are underway for development of a fast river taxi system.

In Portland today, there are so many more places to go and so many ways of getting there: bus, light rail, streetcar, taxi, boat, bicycle, jogging, walking, and, of course, the private automobile.

But beware: the car is fast losing favor with many environmentally sensitive citizens who want to guard against traffic gridlock. They insist Portland's livability be preserved. More and more Portlanders of all ages are looking to other transportation options. More than 380 employers in the Portland area provide transit subsidies to over 150,000 regional employees in an aggressive effort to keep more cars off Portland streets, roads, and highways.

Portland is one of the most bike-friendly cities in the nation. The Oregon Legislature passed the Bike Bill in 1971 to lead the nation in making public roads safe and accessible to bikers. A minimum of one percent of all transportation budgets must include provisions for bike lanes. The City of Portland, with 200 miles of bikeways, a total that increases every year, adds bike lanes when major streets are re-paved. Most of the city's eight bridges are also bicycle-friendly.

Joggers, hikers, and walkers find Portland a Mecca. Parks are found in all sections of the city. Portland's exciting and extensive trail systems cannot be surpassed or equaled. Also impressive is the 40-mile loop trail and the new Springwater Trail.

What makes Portland's parks system unique among U.S. cities is Forest Park, a 5,000-acre pristine forest that covers the face of the city's West Hills offering miles of hiking and jogging trails with occasional glimpses through the trees of the city below.

Portland's livability, combined with its many transportation options, make it an excellent place to site a new business. The city at the foot of Forest Park is also the Pacific Northwest's leading transportation and distribution center, and the tenth-ranked seaport in the U.S.

PART OF THE INTEGRATED TRI-MET TRI-COUNTY TRANSIT SYSTEM, MAX, PORTLAND'S LIGHT RAIL SYSTEM, CONNECTS NEIGHBORHOODS WITH MAJOR EMPLOYMENT CENTERS, REGIONAL SHOPPING, AND ENTERTAINMENT FACILITIES, REDUCING AUTOMOBILE POLLUTION, AND DEFERRING THE NEED FOR NEW HIGHWAY INVESTMENT. A 5.8-MILE SEGMENT WILL SOON CONNECT THE EXPO CENTER IN NORTH PORTLAND WITH DOWNTOWN, AND THE REST OF THE TRANSIT SYSTEM. *PHOTO BY STEVE TERRILL*

THE VINTAGE TROLLEY TAKES PASSENGERS ON A 40-MINUTE TRIP FROM ONE OF MORE THAN 3,000 RETAIL AND PROFESSIONAL BUSINESSES DOWN-TOWN TO THE LLOYD CENTER EVERY HALF HOUR—AND IT'S FREE! *PHOTO BY LARRY GEDDIS*

The Port of Portland, steward of Portland's vast world seaport, actively pursues and promotes freight mobility projects that speed the flow of trains and trucks, benefiting motorists and pedestrians alike. The Port also has done an outstanding job providing fast and uncongested access to its marine terminals and PDX.

Portland started coming of age in the 1880s, when the transcontinental railroads recognized that the low-cost water-grade route of the Columbia River to Portland was the most energy-efficient rail route to the Pacific Coast.

Today, because of its strategic location at the confluence of the Willamette and Columbia Rivers, and its excellent rail service, Portland is the largest wheat port in the U.S.; the fifth largest import/export auto port in the country; and the second largest export port on the West Coast–second only to the huge Los Angeles/Long Beach area.

Portland is a strong regional container port, drawing a quarter of its export containers by barge from Lewiston, Idaho, 365 miles distant on the Snake River; Pasco,

Washington; and Morrow and Umatilla, Oregon on the Columbia River. The Port of Portland's Terminal 6 container complex is the hub for these developing river ports.

The logistical advantages that have made Portland the leading distribution center on the Pacific Coast have also made Portland a truck-friendly center with more than 100 trucking companies operating here. Portland's status as a major export port greatly benefits Portland truckers by offering more back-haul opportunities than found at other West Coast ports.

Portland International Airport, the fastest-growing major U.S. airport during the first half of the 1990s, handled 13.8 million passengers and 252,535 short tons of air freight during 2000. Some 18 passenger carriers and 14 cargo carriers serve PDX with flights to 105 U.S. cities in addition to international service to 12 cities.

Yes, Ben Holladay, we've come a long way since your horse-cars followed the tracks along the riverbank on First Avenue. And it's been well over 100 years since anyone worried about "getting out of the mud." ■

In Portland today, there are so many more places to go and so many ways of getting there.

BUILT IN 1896, PORTLAND'S REFURBISHED, HISTORIC UNION STATION IS LOCATED NEAR THE GREYHOUND BUS DEPOT IN NORTHWEST PORTLAND, PROVIDING A DOWNTOWN PASSENGER SERVICE TRANSPORTATION HUB. AMTRAK SERVES THE PRIMARY NORTH-SOUTH AND EAST-WEST ROUTES OUT OF PORTLAND. *PHOTO LEFT BY LARRY GEDDIS, PHOTO BELOW BY STEVE TERRILL*

Portland's livability and many transportation options make it an excellent place to site a new business.

ONE OF PORTLAND'S BUSIEST BRIDGES, THE TWO-LEVEL MARQUAM BRIDGE, WAS COMPLETED IN 1966. *PHOTO BY STEVE TERRILL*

"At Azumano, we believe that it is important for the community to view itself in the context of a global perspective. Our international connections contribute significantly to the quality of life and the positive business environment that has led to Portland becoming a world-class city. The long-term health of our economy here depends on the citizens and the business community, and if we strive to keep a global perspective it will enhance our ability to remain economically competitive."

Sho Dozono
President and Owner
Azumano Travel

THE PORT OF PORTLAND'S TERMINAL 6 IS SERVED BY THE COLUMBIA/SNAKE RIVER SYSTEM, SECOND LARGEST INLAND WATERWAY IN THE NATION, FROM AS FAR UPRIVER AS LEWISTON, IDAHO. *PHOTO BY STEVE TERRILL* OPPOSITE PAGE: AN EARLY MORNING PORTLAND SKYLINE AND THE HAWTHORNE BRIDGE ARE REFLECTED IN THE WILLAMETTE RIVER, AS SEEN FROM ITS EAST BANK. *PHOTO BY LARRY GEDDIS*

RIGHT: PART OF
THE PORTLAND
INTERNATIONAL AIRPORT
EXPANSION, THIS SEVEN-
STORY-HIGH GLASS
CANOPY OPENED IN JUNE
OF 2000, AND PROTECTS
VISITORS FROM THE
WEATHER. *PHOTO BY
LARRY GEDDIS*

BOTTOM: PORTLANDERS
CAN TAKE MAX TO
THE AIRPORT. THE
5.5-MILE AIRPORT
MAX EXTENSION WAS
THE RESULT OF AN
INNOVATIVE PUBLIC/
PRIVATE VENTURE
BETWEEN THE PORT OF
PORTLAND, TRI-MET,
THE CITY OF PORTLAND,
PORTLAND DEVELOPMENT
COMMISSION, AND
BECHTEL ENTERPRISES,
RESULTING IN NO
ADDITIONAL PROPERTY
TAX DOLLARS,
STATE GENERAL
FUNDS, OR FEDERAL
APPROPRIATIONS.
AIRPORT MAX IS PART
OF THE OVERALL
INTEGRATED TRI-COUNTY
TRANSIT SYSTEM.
*PHOTO COURTESY
OF TRI-MET*
OPPOSITE PAGE:
PORTLAND'S EVENING
COMMUTE BECOMES A
SWIRL OF LIGHTS ALONG
HIGHWAY 26, WEST OF
THE CITY, AS SEEN FROM
ATOP THE VISTA RIDGE
TUNNEL. *PHOTO BY
LARRY GEDDIS*

CHAPTER SEVEN

BY LUCY Z. MARTIN

Health Care

THE COST OF HEALTH CARE IN PORTLAND IS COMPARATIVELY LOW, WHILE QUALITY OF CARE IS HIGH. AN OCTOBER 2000 FEDERAL HEALTH CARE FINANCING ADMINISTRATION EVALUATION OF TWENTY-FOUR QUALITY INDICATORS IN SIX CLINICAL AREAS RANKED OREGON IN THE TOP 25 PERCENT OF ALL STATES. *PHOTO COURTESY OF KAISER PERMANENTE*

Progressive, comprehensive, collaborative—when the subject is health care in Portland, these are the words that crop up time and again.

And with good reason.

While the state is known as a trendsetter in health-care policy—witness the national stir caused by both the Oregon Health Plan and our assisted suicide law—Portland is also a national leader in providing high-quality care at comparatively low rates.

A referral center, the city offers extraordinary access to a range of sophisticated services. Whether the need is for burn treatment, specialized pediatric care, an organ transplant, or cancer therapy, a wealth of traditional medical options is available.

And the health-care choices don't end there. As a training center for naturopaths, massage therapists, chiropractors, and acupuncturists, Portland offers a comprehensive selection of complementary care opportunities, as well.

As in other metropolitan areas around the nation, competition for health-care dollars can be intense in Portland. And yet, health-care providers here place a premium on the community's well-being. This concern for the community is the source of numerous collaborations, including joint research projects and the sharing of costly

equipment. Whatever the effort, the intent is clear—to provide the community with the best health-care options available.

When compared with other states in the nation, spending on health care in Oregon ranks relatively low. Undoubtedly, managed care plays a role in keeping costs down.

Portland's first experience with managed care was in the 1940s when Henry J. Kaiser founded what is known today as Kaiser Permanente in his West Coast shipyards. When the war ended, the Kaiser health plan was opened to the public.

Today, when only 36 percent of the national population is enrolled in managed care, nearly half (49 percent) of Portlanders are enrolled in a managed care plan—one of the highest rates in the nation.

And while the cost of care in Portland remains comparatively low, the quality of care is high. In October 2000, Oregon ranked in the top 25 percent of all states in an evaluation of twenty-four quality indicators in six clinical areas conducted by the Health Care Financing Administration.

The Portland metropolitan area is home to eighteen hospitals, most of them nonprofit and associated with one of the three largest health-care delivery systems: Legacy Health System, Providence Health System, and Kaiser Permanente.

Legacy Health System has four hospitals: Legacy Emanuel Hospital and Health Center, Legacy Good

OPPOSITE PAGE: PORTLANDERS SUPPORT CHARITIES WITH A VARIETY OF FUNDRAISING EVENTS. SUMMERTIME RUNS ARE VERY POPULAR, AND FREQUENTLY INCLUDE WALKING EVENTS AS WELL. MORE THAN 2,500 RUNNERS PARTICIPATE IN THE ANNUAL JUNE RIVER CITY DISTANCE CLASSIC. *PHOTO BY LARRY GEDDIS*

Portland is a national leader in providing high-quality care at comparatively low rates.

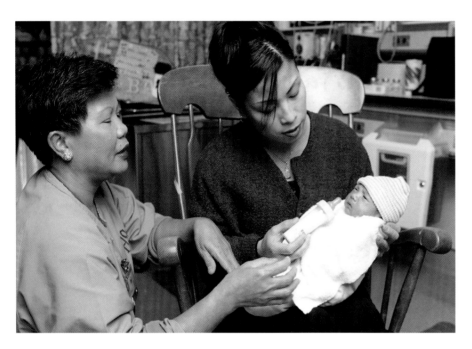

Oregon Health & Science University (OHSU), the state's only academic health center, Portland's largest employer, and the area's leader in biotechnology, includes both OHSU Hospital and Doernbecher Children's Hospital. Doernbecher offers a wide range of pediatric services to more than 35,000 children each year from Oregon and five surrounding states. The Veterans Affairs Medical Center is located nearby, as well.

OHSU is internationally known for developing nonsurgical treatments to open blocked blood vessels, shrink tumors, stop internal bleeding, and correct infertility, and is also noted for its neuroscience and biotechnology expertise. OHSU's gynecology and kidney disease specialty treatment services rank among the nation's best, according to surveys by *US News & World Report*. OHSU not only has a medical school and a nursing school, but also the state's only dental school.

Other area hospitals include Tuality Community Hospital in Hillsboro; Willamette Falls Hospital in Oregon City; and, in Portland, Adventist Medical Center, Eastmoreland Hospital, Shriners Hospital for Children, Woodland Park Hospital, and BHC Pacific Gateway Hospital. Across the Columbia River in Vancouver, Washington, is Southwest Washington Medical Center, the area's fifth-largest hospital, with its two campuses.

While Portland is widely recognized for its traditional medical facilities, Portland residents also have ready access to an abundance of complementary care providers. *Natural Health* magazine named the City of Roses fourth among the nation's "natural healthiest" places to live, in part because of the high ratio of area residents to acupuncturists.

In fact, as home to the Oregon College of Oriental Medicine (OCOM), a non-profit, nationally accredited educational institution founded in 1983, Portland is a training center for acupuncturists. OCOM is approved by the State of Oregon and confers a master's degree in acupuncture and Oriental medicine.

In addition, Portland is home to the nation's oldest naturopathic college, the National College of Naturopathic Medicine (NCNM), which was established here in 1956. An active member of the community, NCNM runs three clinics and services twelve additional community clinics that offer free or low-cost care.

With two schools of massage based in Portland, the city is also a training ground for massage therapists. The East-West College of Healing Arts, accredited by the Commission on

Samaritan Hospital and Medical Center, Legacy Meridian Park Hospital, and Legacy Mount Hood Medical Center.

Based at Emanuel, Legacy's Oregon Burn Center is the only facility of its kind between Seattle and San Francisco, and is a leader and innovator in burn assessment, treatment, and rehabilitation. Legacy Emanuel Children's Hospital, the largest children's hospital in Oregon, boasts a state-of-the-art treatment center. Legacy Good Samaritan is also recognized as providing outstanding cardiovascular services.

Providence has three hospitals in the Portland area: Providence St. Vincent Medical Center, Providence Portland Medical Center, and Providence Milwaukie Hospital. Providence's Women and Children's Program is devoted to improving the health of women and children, and collaborates with other Providence Health System programs to provide a complete range of health-care services for women of all ages. With 527 babies born at St. Vincent in July 2000 alone, Providence delivers the most babies in the state.

The Providence Heart Institute is internationally renowned as a leader in cardiac care, research, and education. Providence's Earle A. Chiles Research Institute is noted for developing new strategies for both cardiac and cancer care.

Kaiser has one hospital, Sunnyside Medical Center in Clackamas, plus twenty outpatient medical offices and fifteen dental offices. Kaiser also maintains a cooperative agreement with a number of area hospitals for inpatient services for members.

Massage Therapy Accreditation, has been an educational center for massage therapists for thirty years.

The Oregon School of Massage, founded in 1984, is a private professional school devoted to massage and related health education, and is licensed by the Oregon Department of Education.

Western States Chiropractic College (WSCC), whose roots reach back to the early twentieth century, is also located in Portland. One of nineteen chiropractic colleges in North America, WSCC was the first chiropractic college in the nation ever awarded a federal grant for research. In 1994, that grant, from the Department of Health and Human Services, funded a collaborative study with OHSU's Department of Family Medicine. A second grant was awarded more recently to continue and expand that original research.

Collaboration, such as that between OHSU and WSCC, is a hallmark of health care in Portland. Another cooperative research effort finds the Kaiser Center for Health Research working with the Oregon College of Oriental Medicine on complementary and alternative treatments for TMD and periodontal disease, through a grant from the National Center for Complementary and Alternative Medicine of the National Institutes of Health. OCOM also is working with OHSU's Neurology Department to explore alternative approaches for treating neurodegenerative disorders such as Alzheimer's and multiple sclerosis.

Portland providers have taken an aggressive approach in combining resources to provide services to the community that might not otherwise exist. Oregon Health Systems in Collaboration (OHSIC) pulls together a number of large providers and insurers to create a public/private partnership focused on seeking solutions to community problems. For example, the group has developed a vaccination registry, unique in that it is the only statewide registry of its kind in the nation.

As both a trendsetter and a sophisticated educational resource, Portland manages to keep an eye on the future while at the same time remaining committed to meeting the community's present health-care needs. Aggressive in collaborating, progressive in acting, and comprehensive in nature—the city's commitment has made it a health-care model for the nation. ∎

MANAGED CARE CAME TO PORTLAND IN THE 1940'S, WHEN KAISER PERMANENTE'S MEDICAL GROUP PROVIDED SERVICES TO KAISER SHIPYARDS WORKERS. TODAY, NEARLY HALF OF PORTLAND'S RESIDENTS ARE ENROLLED IN A MANAGED CARE HEALTH PLAN, ONE OF THE HIGHEST RATES IN THE COUNTRY. *PHOTO COURTESY OF KAISER PERMANENTE*

RIGHT: OHSU HAS THE OLDEST AND MOST COMPREHENSIVE SOLID ORGAN TRANSPLANT PROGRAM IN OREGON, AND WAS THE FIRST IN THE STATE TO PERFORM HEART, KIDNEY, LIVER, LUNG, AND PANCREAS TRANSPLANTS. OHSU'S CARDIAC PROGRAM IS A REGIONAL RESOURCE FOR BOTH ADULT AND PEDIATRIC CARDIAC CARE. NATIONALLY-RECOGNIZED CARDIAC PHYSICIANS AVERAGE MORE THAN 1,100 PROCEDURES EACH YEAR. *PHOTO BY DON HAMILTON/ COURTESY OF OHSU*

BOTTOM: OHSU'S EMERGENCY DEPARTMENT AND ITS LEVEL I TRAUMA CENTER HAS BEEN NATIONALLY RECOGNIZED BY TRAUMA EXPERTS AS ONE OF THE NATION'S PREMIER TRAUMA CENTERS AS DETERMINED BY PATIENT OUTCOMES. THE EMERGENCY DEPARTMENT OF OREGON'S MEDICAL RESOURCE HOSPITAL IS THE REGIONAL TRANSPORTATION TELECOMMUNICATION CENTER FOR ANY MASS CASUALTY OR DISASTER, DIRECTING LIFE FLIGHT, AMBULANCE, AND EMERGENCY MEDICAL CALLS. *PHOTO BY DON HAMILTON/COURTESY OF OHSU*

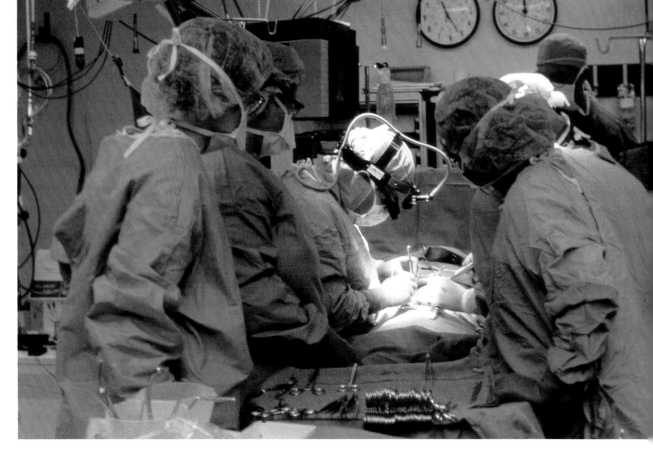

Health-care providers here place a premium on the community's well-being.

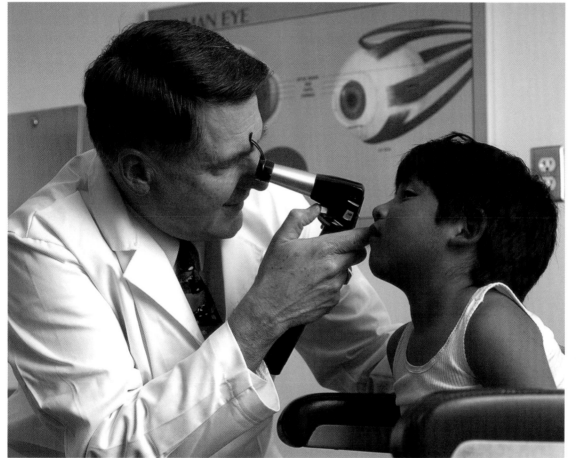

DOERNBECHER CHILDREN'S HOSPITAL PROVIDES THE WIDEST RANGE OF HEALTH-CARE SERVICES TO CHILDREN IN THE REGION, CARING FOR MORE THAN 38,000 EACH YEAR AT A NEW STATE-OF-THE-ART PEDIATRIC MEDICAL COMPLEX. NATIONALLY RECOGNIZED, DOERNBECHER PROVIDES APPROXIMATELY 70 PERCENT OF ALL PEDIATRIC CANCER CARE IN OREGON, AND IS THE PRIMARY SOURCE FOR UNIQUE CLINICAL SERVICES SUCH AS SOLID ORGAN AND BONE MARROW TRANSPLANTATION. DOERNBECHER ALSO OFFERS HIGHLY ADVANCED CARE FOR HEART AND KIDNEY DISEASE, ENDOCRINE DISORDERS, GENETIC ABNORMALITIES, SERIOUS INJURIES, AND COMPLICATIONS FROM PREMATURE BIRTH. *PHOTO COURTESY OF OHSU*

"As Oregon's only academic health center, OHSU is a unique resource for all Oregonians. In just the past five years, OHSU has undergone a dramatic transformation from a state agency to a dynamic public corporation. Building for the future, OHSU is in the middle of a major expansion of its research programs. Oregonians across the state will benefit from increased access to quality health care and a growing industry based on OHSU ideas and innovations."

Peter O. Kohler, M.D.
President
Oregon Health & Science University

Portland keeps an eye on the future and remains committed to the community's health-care needs.

PLACING A PREMIUM ON THE COMMUNITY'S WELL-BEING, HEALTH-CARE PROVIDERS COLLABORATE ON JOINT RESEARCH PROJECTS, AND SHARE EXPENSIVE EQUIPMENT TO KEEP COSTS LOW. *PHOTO COURTESY OF KAISER PERMANENTE*

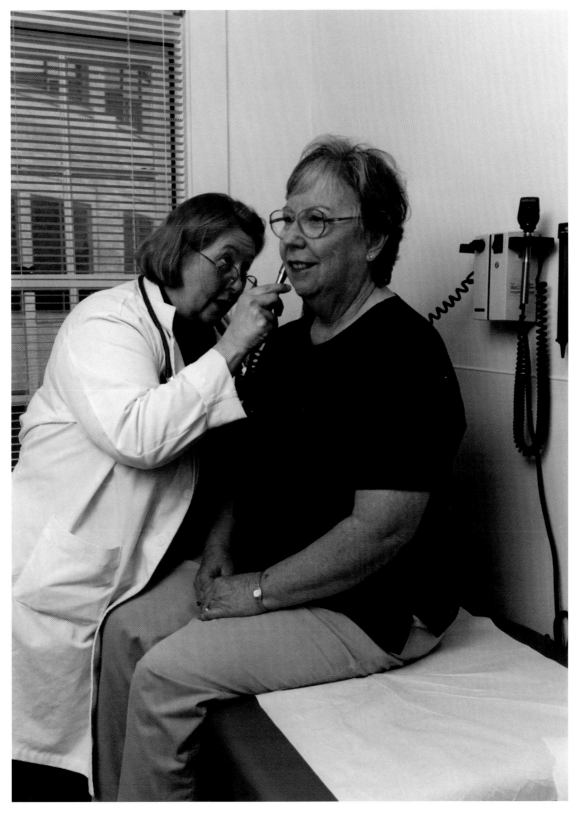

OREGON HEALTH & SCIENCE UNIVERSITY'S SCHOOL OF NURSING GRADUATE PROGRAMS ARE RANKED IN THE TOP TWO PERCENT FOR EXCELLENCE AND QUALITY AS REPORTED IN *U.S. NEWS & WORLD REPORT*. RANKED TENTH NATIONALLY BY THE NATIONAL INSTITUTE OF HEALTH (NIH) FOR RESEARCH FUNDING, THE SCHOOL HAS PIONEERED DISTANCE-LEARNING PROGRAMS, IN ADDITION TO ITS ON-CAMPUS CLASSES. *PHOTO BY BRUCE BEATON/COURTESY OF OHSU*

CHAPTER EIGHT

BY KATHY WATSON

The Vibrant Economy

Before Bill Bowerman created the first Nike running shoe on a waffle iron, before Intel located its world's largest campus here, before the city's long, wide boulevards flowed east and west across the Willamette River connecting commerce and education and housing in a graceful economic ballet, even before timber and agriculture brought prosperity to Portland, there were Lewis and Clark.

The great explorers, who floated through the area nearly 200 years ago in search of the Pacific Ocean, were struck by the region's potential. In his journal, Meriwether Lewis wrote that the area "would be competent to the maintenance of forty or fifty thousand souls if properly cultivated."

Oh, how right he was, though he misjudged things a bit.

Today, the six-county Portland metro region is home to some 1.9 million souls. Though the city still claims the sort of cultivation Lewis might recognize—farmer's markets, breweries, and wineries—it is cultivation of another sort that has drawn so many here since the Corps of Discovery passed through.

The city has cultivated first and foremost a diversified economy. How diverse? Major transportation equipment companies such as railcar maker Greenbrier and truck manufacturer Freightliner. Start-up life sciences companies supported by Oregon Health & Science University and its research dollars—$167 million in 1999 alone. A vital tourism industry. A growing cluster of music, film and video, and entertainment companies tapping into new technologies in the wireless and networked world.

You could say Portland has two spines. There's the traditional backbone built on inexpensive power, vast forests, fertile soil, and a diverse fishery. That spine today still supports healthy natural resource industries, keeping the Port of Portland one of the busiest on the West Coast. Five of Portland's top ten public companies and five of its top ten private companies are built on Oregon's natural resources.

The second spine, sprouted in the early 1980s, is now the backbone of a technology explosion. A May 2000 study by the American Electronics Association (AeA) ranked Oregon as the fourth highest in U.S. high-tech job growth, adding nearly 27,000 technology jobs between 1993 and 1998. Oregon also ranked fourth in semiconductor employment, after California, Texas, and Arizona. Overall, Oregon ranks nineteenth in the nation for high-tech employment, and sixteenth in technology wages. Technology is Oregon's largest manufacturing industry, highest paying industry, and largest exporter. And Portland is technology's heart and soul.

Combined, these two spines mean that Oregon is the second leading export state in the nation, with technology headlining the marquee.

And while we can certainly boast our technology name brands–from Hewlett Packard to Intel, Tektronix, and InFocus, the last five years have seen an explosion in Oregon startups, as well. The state is now seventh in the nation for creation of new companies, with signs that it might blast even higher in the years ahead.

What's generating all the new company growth? For years, Portlanders watched as Silicon Valley to the south and Seattle to the north became startup boom towns where the venture capital flowed, and where new millionaires made substantial investments in the local universities and in subsequent startups.

But Portland is now flexing its muscle as a high-tech center. Even when the economy cools on the entire West Coast, Portland's entrepreneurial environment tends to keep our economy on an even keel.

One of the best indicators of this steady economic climate is the amount of venture capital invested here. "From a venture perspective, this is one of the hottest markets on the West Coast," says Derek Ridgley, vice president of Silicon Valley Bank's Portland-area office. "We see a lot of investors visiting the Oregon market looking for more substantial deals than they're finding in other markets."

Silicon Valley bank (SVB) noted an astounding $600 million of institutional venture capital investment in Oregon companies in 2000, extending a strong growth trend for venture capital in the state. In 1999, Oregon received more than $400 million in such investments–double the amount received in the previous four years combined, and roughly ten times the amount received in 1998.

Now, groups such as the Oregon Angel Network crowd sixty investors together in a member's living room each month to see new company presentations. Local venture firms like SmartForest Ventures and Venture Mechanics are not only investing in startups, they're providing critical early-stage brainpower. Venture Mechanics even provides the companies it assists with executive SWAT teams, turning the incubator idea on its head.

The Oregon Entrepreneurs Forum, over 1,200 members strong, is creating a lush, welcoming environment to nurture startups. Community support for business abounds.

The area's universities, both public and private, are experiencing a sort of renaissance, capturing millions in grants and spinning out new companies and technologies at a much higher rate than in years past. The nexus of computer engineering and genomics is driving an exciting new area of research involving Portland's engineering schools and its medical school.

The pool of talented executives is growing, too, giving rise to home-grown teams launching category-winning companies.

"Oregon now has several industry areas that are described as 'fly-wheels,'" Ridgley explains. "They spin out people and technology. We're starting to see a lot of second-generation entrepreneurs."

Portland has cultivated first and foremost a diversified economy.

THE FOURTH LARGEST DEEP-WATER PORT ON THE WEST COAST, THE PORT OF PORTLAND OPERATES FOUR MARINE TERMINALS ACCOMMO-DATING CONTAINER SHIPS, GRAIN VESSELS, BREAKBULK, AND AUTO CARRIERS. *PHOTO BY STEVE TERRILL*

THE COLUMBIA RIVER'S BUSY BARGE TRAFFIC BRINGS A VARIETY OF BULK AND CONTAINERIZED CARGO TO PORT OF PORTLAND DOCKS FOR EXPORT TO ASIA, AUSTRALIA, NEW ZEALAND, SOUTH AMERICA, AND THE MEDITERRANEAN. *PHOTO BY STEVE TERRILL*

Take Steve Wood, for example. He built Surplus Direct to $100 million in sales, and then sold it to Egghead Software. He and his friends, experienced executives with an ear for good music, bought local Django Music. Then they began creating a nationwide kingdom of used-music stores under the brand Django.com. Heaped high with new technology and e-commerce, Django.com saw sales in six months rocket to $12 million–and counting.

Or take Ron Weiner, who built printbid.com, sold it to ImageX.com for $23.5 million, and turned right around to start SnapNames.com, a company that allows people to snatch up URLs,Web site names, as they expire, or to protect their own brands.

And it's all happening in downtown Portland. The growth of new business is carving yet another upward growth curve into the commercial real estate and construction industries. The occupancy rate for office space in the downtown central business district is 94 percent, one of the healthiest in the country.

The pool of talented executives is growing, giving rise to category-winning companies.

IN SUPPORT OF THE CITY'S COMMITMENT TO A HEALTHY ENVIRONMENT, PORTLANDERS ENJOY EXCELLENT TRANSPORTATION ALTERNATIVES TO THE AUTOMOBILE. WITH THEIR DAILY SERVICE AREA OF NEARLY 600 SQUARE MILES, TRI-MET BUSES ARE FULLY ACCESSIBLE TO PEOPLE WITH DISABILITIES. "FARELESS SQUARE"— THE DOWNTOWN AREA WHERE PASSENGERS RIDE FREE—HAS RECENTLY BEEN EXPANDED TO INCLUDE THE LLOYD DISTRICT, OREGON CONVENTION CENTER, AND ROSE QUARTER ON THE EAST SIDE OF THE WILLAMETTE RIVER.
PHOTO BY STEVE TERRILL

FROM MANUFACTURING TO TECHNOLOGY, PORTLAND HAS CULTIVATED ITS DIVERSE ECONOMY TO BE A BUTTRESS AGAINST UNCERTAIN ECONOMIC CONDITIONS. *PHOTO BY STEVE TERRILL*

There is an energy that feeds new and established companies alike: the exchange of ideas, the proximity to good living. Portland's downtown is home to 1.4 million square feet of shopping and dining, keeping the city alive until late each night. Yet it is also close to parks and wilderness and closely-knit neighborhoods. New residents are responding to Portland's attraction. A 1999 state study showed that quality of life surpasses the combined appeal of jobs and company transfers as reasons people move to Oregon. And of those who moved as a result of a job offer or company transfer, 37 percent cite quality of life as an additional contributing factor.

Life and work combined make Portland's economy a dynamo. Lewis and Clark should have stayed. ■

JUST ACROSS THE RIVER FROM DOWNTOWN, THE THRIVING LLOYD CENTER WAS THE FIRST MAJOR MALL IN OREGON, AND REMAINS THE LARGEST. ITS QUALITY SHOPS, STORES, AND RESTAURANTS SURROUND A YEAR-ROUND INDOOR ICE-SKATING RINK. *PHOTO BY STEVE TERRILL*

There is an energy that feeds companies: the exchange of ideas, the proximity to good living.

RIGHT: LATE EVENING LIGHT SHINES ON A FIELD OF RED APELDOORN TULIPS AT THE WOODEN SHOE BULB COMPANY IN WOODBURN, OREGON, LESS THAN AN HOUR FROM PORTLAND. MORE THAN 160 VARIETIES ARE GROWN ON THIRTY ACRES, AND THE PUBLIC IS INVITED TO VISIT THE COLORFUL SHOW EACH SPRING. *PHOTO BY LARRY GEDDIS*

BOTTOM: OVERLOOKING THE WILLAMETTE RIVER AT THE UNIVERSITY OF PORTLAND, A STATUE OF WILLIAM CLARK COMMEMORATES HIS 1806 VISIT TO THIS SIGHT. *PHOTO BY LARRY GEDDIS*

OPPOSITE PAGE: PRESERVING THE ENVIRONMENT WHILE BUILDING FOR GROWTH HAS LONG BEEN A PORTLAND VALUE. THANKS TO AREA RESIDENTS, 641-ACRE TRYON CREEK STATE PARK, A PRE-HISTORY SITE WITH ABUNDANT GAME AND VEGETATION SUPPORTING INDIGENOUS PEOPLES, WAS RECLAIMED FROM NINETEENTH-CENTURY INDUSTRIAL USE DURING THE 1970S. TODAY, THIS STATE PARK OFFERS 8 MILES OF HIKING TRAILS, 3.5 MILES OF HORSE TRAILS, AND 3 MILES OF BICYCLE TRAILS FOR YEAR-ROUND USE. *PHOTO BY LARRY GEDDIS*

"IDT achieved record financial results in fiscal 2001. Revenues were $992 million, up 41 percent from 2000, and net income was $3.76 per share. Strong volume growth and superior products in the Communications, High Performance Logic, and SRAMs and Other product segments, together with our efficient cost structure, resulted in all-time highs for revenues, gross margin, and operating income. This marked a great year of progress for IDT as well as its shareholders."

C.Y. Chen
Managing Director, Oregon Operations
IDT (Integrated Device Technology)

CHAPTER NINE

BY KYLE RITCHEY-NOLL

Oregon's Silicon Forest

Forests have long been the heritage and the future of Oregon's economy. Early pioneers arrived in the state and found trees in abundance. They built a thriving lumber and wood products industry. Today, Oregon's economy is driven not so much by trees, but by the forest–The Silicon Forest, a vibrant high-technology industry. With unparalleled growth, Oregon's technology industry surpassed lumber and wood products in the mid-1990s and is now the state's fastest growing and largest industry.

The roots of Oregon's Silicon Forest stretch back more than half a century. The industry began in the 1940s with small local firms, such as Electro Scientific Industries (then Brown Engineering) and Tektronix. These businesses grew into leading technology enterprises and helped form the critical mass of technology and talent that gave birth to Oregon's leading industry.

During the 1970s, major technology companies began to look outside the borders of California to expand and relocate. Oregon was fortunate to attract several anchor tenants during this time. In 1975, Hewlett-Packard moved to Corvallis in the Willamette Valley, and Intel arrived in Washington County's Aloha (west of Portland) in 1976. Growth continued throughout the 1980s, as venture capital flowed into the state and second generation or spin-off companies flourished. More

than 170 startup companies were formed in Oregon between 1980 and 1986. A large number of multinational firms, many from Japan, also relocated to Oregon during this decade. The Silicon Forest was born.

With Oregon on the technology roadmap, technology executives began to recognize the obvious: Oregon's people, pure water, quality of life, and location made it an ideal place to do business.

Portland's infrastructure, access to global markets, rich talent pool, and quality of life make it one of the best places for technology companies in the country, said Allen Alley, president & CEO of Pixelworks, a Tualatin semiconductor-design company, and 2001 chairman of the Oregon Council of American Electronics Association, the nation's largest high-tech trade association.

Today, Oregon's $22 billion high-tech industry is highly diversified, with world-class leaders in computers, semiconductors, software, instruments, printers, displays, communications, and consumer electronics. Such industry giants as Intel, Hewlett-Packard, LSI Logic, Sony, IBM, Xerox, and Tektronix have operations in Oregon, but most of the nearly 1,700 technology firms in the state are small, entrepreneurial businesses, with half being less than ten years old and 22 percent less than three years old.

Portland is a solid technology community because it is so broadly diversified.

Portland is a solid technology community because it is so broadly diversified, from Internet companies to IC manufacturers, stated Keith Barnes, chairman and CEO of Integrated Measurement Systems, a Beaverton-based manufacturer of test verification equipment.

While the Silicon Forest's old growth is in the Portland area, certainly the forest has spread throughout Oregon. Traditionally, 80 percent of the state's technology industry has been clustered around the Portland metropolitan area; however, the industry is expanding in such areas as Bend, Salem, Eugene, Corvallis, and Southern Oregon. From farmers in Eastern Oregon using global positioning technology to guide their planting, to Harry & David in Medford using the Internet to distribute fresh pears worldwide, technology is driving the state's economy.

Nearly 73,000 Oregonians are employed in the technology industry today, with more than 64,000 in the Portland metropolitan area. According to AeA's *Cybercities* report, a city-by-city overview of the high-tech industry, employment in the Portland metro area has grown more than 53 percent since 1993 alone, adding 22,200 new jobs, and ranking the region as the tenth fastest-growing metropolitan area in the

United States. These tech employees earn an average wage of $60,000, which is nearly 80 percent more than the average private sector wage in the state.

The semiconductor industry remains the largest industry segment, representing about one-third of the state's total high-tech employment. The expansion and relocation in the 1990s of many of the world's leading and emerging semiconductor firms, such as Intel, Fujitsu, Wacker Siltronic, LSI Logic, TriQuint Semiconductor, and IDT, helped rank the Portland area as the nation's fourth largest cybercity in semiconductor manufacturing employment behind San Jose, Phoenix, and Dallas. Indeed, it comes as a surprise to many to learn that Intel's Oregon site is its largest in the world, in terms of employment and square footage.

While semiconductors have led job creation in the last decade, the software and computer services segment is the fastest growing, adding 1,800 new jobs a year, according to the *2000 AeA Oregon Technology Benchmarks Report.* Mentor Graphics, ABC Technologies, and Timberline Software rank among the state's largest software companies. Without a sales tax, Oregon has been a fertile environment for the growth of Internet retail firms. The state also is home to a

PRIVATE SECTOR INDUSTRY ACTIVELY SUPPORTS RESEARCH PROGRAMS AND FACILITIES IN PARTNERSHIP WITH PORTLAND-AREA COLLEGES AND UNIVERSITIES. SPONSORED BY CREDENCE SYSTEMS CORPORATION, THIS FACILITY IS AT PORTLAND STATE UNIVERSITY. *PHOTO BY JERRY HART/COURTESY OF PORTLAND STATE UNIVERSITY*

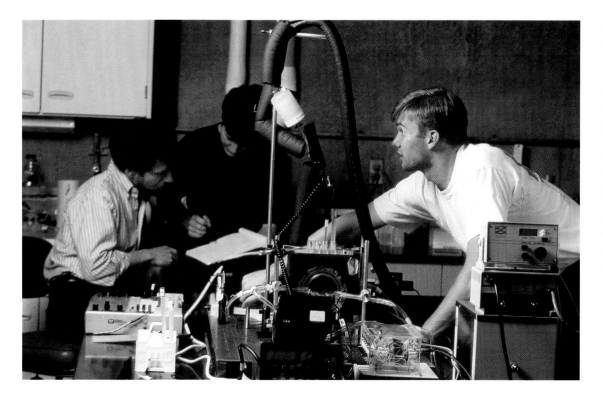

THE TECHNOLOGY
INDUSTRY HAS LONG
CHAMPIONED HIGHER
EDUCATION IN THE
SILICON FOREST.
MANY COLLEGES AND
UNIVERSITIES IN THE
PORTLAND AREA OFFER
SPECIALIZED CURRICULA
DESIGNED TO PREPARE
STUDENTS, SUCH AS
THESE AT LEWIS &
CLARK COLLEGE, FOR
TECHNOLOGY CAREERS.
*PHOTO COURTESY OF
LEWIS & CLARK COLLEGE*

number of firms that are building tools for the Internet, such as Webridge, Step Technology, and Webtrends.

Technology products also have become Oregon's leading export crop. High-tech exports totaled $5.1 billion in 1999, nearly half of the state's total exports, and more than agriculture and wood products combined. Technology exports have tripled since 1990 as high-tech firms have expanded sales into Europe, the Pacific Rim, and other parts of the world.

Oregonians seem to have embraced the technology revolution. More than 69 percent of all households in the Portland region had a computer in August 2000, ranked third nationwide according to AeA *Cybercities.* Likewise, 58 percent of region households had Internet access, ranked fourth nationwide. Recognizing the key role the Internet plays in the economic and personal lives of Oregonians, the technology industry worked with the 1999 Legislature to create the Oregon Internet Commission to encourage the development of, and access to the Internet.

Oregon's technology industry has long played an active role in state public policy. Advocacy for education, especially higher education, has been the industry's highest priority. Indeed, executives recognized early on that the strength of Oregon's workforce was the most critical factor in the industry's future success. For a knowledge-based industry, well-educated, creative minds are its seed-crop. The industry

is working with higher education officials and state lawmakers to double the number of engineering graduates in the state by 2005, and to develop a top-ranked engineering school in Oregon by 2010.

As the technology industry has matured and gained economic strength, executives more than ever have begun to turn their focus toward giving back to the community. With economic leadership comes responsibility, said Allen Alley. The high-tech community wants to make a positive and lasting contribution by giving back.

Many seem to share Alley's point of view. The industry contributed more than $16.5 million in cash and equipment in 1999. In addition, executives serve on 129 civic boards, and approximately one-third of all technology employees volunteer in community organizations. Three Oregon technology firms–Tektronix, Intel, and Mentor Graphics–have active corporate foundations that contribute to education, civic, or arts organizations. If there's one predominate cause that the industry supports, it is clearly education.

What does the future hold? Oregon technology executives are optimistic about the future. In the *2000 AeA Oregon Technology Benchmarks Report,* executives predicted that over the next three years they would add another 25,000 new jobs, and that industry revenue will expand more than 40 percent. For Oregon's Silicon Forest, the outlook seems to call for continued strong growth ahead. ■

RIGHT: A CLEANROOM WORKER USES THE NEXT GENERATION OF CHIP-MAKING TECHNOLOGY TO TEST A 300MM WAFER AT A LOCAL CHIP TESTING SITE. THE SEMI-CONDUCTOR INDUSTRY IS THE LARGEST AREA INDUSTRY SEGMENT, REPRESENTING ABOUT ONE-THIRD OF THE STATE'S TOTAL HIGH-TECH EMPLOYMENT. *PHOTO COURTESY OF INTEL CORPORATION*

BOTTOM: IN AN ENVIRONMENT MORE STERILE THAN AN OPERATING THEATER, CLEANROOM WORKERS REVIEW OPERATIONAL PROCEDURES TO MAKE SURE NO CONTAMINATION AFFECTS THE FINAL PRODUCT. *PHOTO COURTESY OF INTEL CORPORATION*

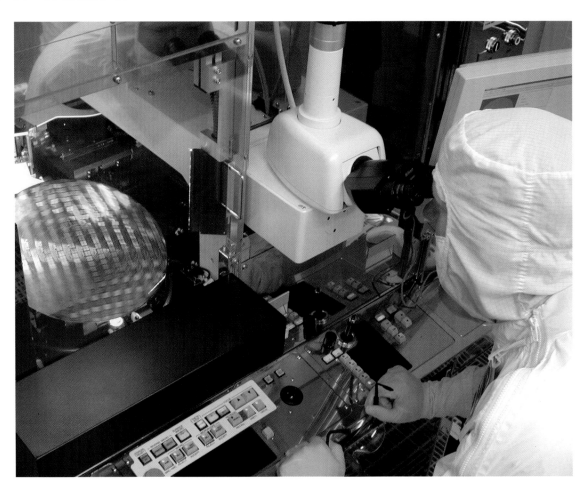

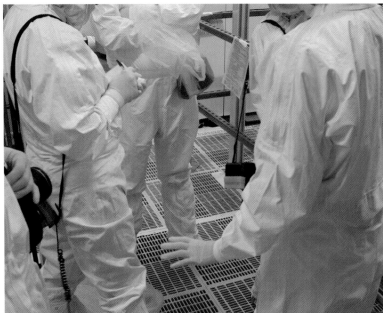

"The IBM campus at Beaverton serves as the headquarters for the Open Source Development Lab–OSDL–an open source Linux development group whose founding partners include IBM, Intel, Computer Associates, Hewlett-Packard, NEC, and a number of others. While not an official part of IBM, the organization contributes significant resources to the venture, believing it to be an important resource for the industry at large and a lure for top talent from around the world."

Rick Warren
Senior Executive
IBM

The strength of Oregon's workforce is the most critical factor in the industry's future success.

TOP: LOCATED IN THE HEART OF OREGON'S SILICON FOREST, AND NAMED AMERICA'S 1998 MASTER-PLANNED COMMUNITY OF THE YEAR BY THE NATIONAL HOME BUILDERS ASSOCIATION, ORENCO STATION IS REMINISCENT OF EARLY-DAY TOWNS AND VILLAGES. THE TOWN CENTER IS A MIX OF FINE RESTAURANTS, SHOPS, AND SERVICES, WITH LOFT RESIDENCES ABOVE. TOWN CENTER TOWNHOMES OFFER STREET-LEVEL PROFESSIONAL OR HOME-BASED BUSINESS OFFICES, WITH LUXURY TOWNHOMES UPSTAIRS. CENTRAL PARK IS SURROUNDED BY A TRADITIONAL NEIGHBOR-HOOD OF SINGLE-FAMILY DETACHED AND ATTACHED HOMES. *PHOTO BY LARRY GEDDIS*

BOTTOM: WELL-EDUCATED, CREATIVE MINDS FOUND IN METROPOLITAN PORTLAND ARE CRITICAL TO OREGON'S TECHNOLOGY INDUSTRY. *PHOTO BY LARRY GEDDIS*

CHAPTER TEN

BY DICK REITEN

Planning for Growth

COMFORTABLE FAMILY NEIGHBORHOODS INCLUDE HOMES IN ALL PRICE RANGES THROUGHOUT THE CITY, INCLUDING THIS ONE IN THE FOREST HEIGHTS AREA OF PORTLAND'S WEST HILLS. *PHOTO BY STEVE TERRILL*

Portlanders have long believed they can shape their own future, and there is plenty of evidence to prove they're right. In so many ways, the quality of life Portland enjoys today is a direct result of choices made in the past. A vibrant downtown, spectacular parks, an envied light rail system and world-class schools–all are products of a visionary citizenry, one deeply committed to the notion that few good things happen by accident.

It is with this legacy that Portland faces its future, and the choices posed by more than a decade of rapid growth. Today, more than ever before, the city must grapple with the results of its own success. Its renowned quality of life has attracted waves of new industries and residents, strengthening the area's economy but challenging the livability that brought them here.

For some communities the situation might be overwhelming; for Portland, it is an opportunity to demonstrate the qualities that set us apart. One of those is clearly the foresight of its public and private sector leaders. At difficult times in its past, our city has been blessed with bold elected leadership and a business community willing to join with them to meet the challenge.

Over the past twenty-five years, government and business worked together to, among other things, renovate downtown,

diversify the region's economy, expand the transit system, build new parks, and create more central city housing. These public-private partnerships have been key to Portland's past success, and today they are a central part of the city's efforts to manage growth.

In Portland, there is a shared view that quality of life and economic vitality reinforce and support one another. This belief guides our planning and helps bring together public and private sector leaders in pursuit of a common agenda. That agenda, simply put, is to build both a prosperous and a livable city. To accomplish this, Portland has assembled a comprehensive array of strategies.

One of the metropolitan area's key strategies for managing growth is to make sure downtown Portland remains a vibrant place where people live as well as work. In the late 1980s, downtown property owners, in partnership with the city, created the Association for Portland Progress to keep the core of the City clean and safe. Today, the Association provides a long list of services and has become one of the nation's most successful business improvement districts.

During the last few years, private business people and city officials have partnered on a host of innovative developments that are transforming former central city industrial areas into new neighborhoods. The Pearl District, River District,

OPPOSITE PAGE: WITH A GROWTH RATE OF 21 PERCENT DURING THE LAST DECADE OF THE TWENTIETH CENTURY, PORTLAND HAS ATTRACTED MANY NEW UNIQUELY PLANNED NEIGHBORHOODS. *PHOTO BY STEVE TERRILL*

There is a shared view that quality of life and economic vitality re-enforce and support one another.

Brewery Blocks, and Old Town Chinatown are coming alive with thousands of units of new condominiums, lofts and apartments, all interwoven with retail and office activities.

There are new redevelopment projects on the drawing boards for North Macadam, just south of the downtown core, and along a new light rail line that will be built on the east side of the river. Portland's central city is thriving, attracting new residents and businesses. And as it prospers, it is helping reduce sprawl at the fringes of our metropolitan area.

The rest of the region also is working hard to shape growth. Mixed-use, transit-oriented developments are sprouting in every part of the metropolitan area. Orenco Station along the Westside light rail line, Canyon Creek Meadows in Clackamas County, and Fairview Village in Multnomah County, are just a few of the projects across the region that are creating complete communities with higher densities, convenient retail services, and more transit options.

These "smart development" projects are helping Portland deal with the increase in cars and commute times created by a growing population. It's one piece of a larger comprehensive transportation planning effort that public and private sector leaders are also working on together. Their goal is to keep people and goods moving smoothly and efficiently throughout the metropolitan area.

This public-private transportation partnership is delivering results. We have moved forward on two expansions of the region's light rail system—one to the airport and the other through North Portland. A new streetcar line has been built through the downtown core, financed in part by property owners along the route. And more targeted planning efforts are underway to help make sure the region's key freight corridors can operate efficiently as we grow.

Portland is in many ways defined by its parks and open space. They serve as a testament to our belief that environmental quality and economic vitality are mutually supportive. But the region's continued growth is testing our commitment to making sure parks and open space keep pace with development. So far, we are meeting the challenge. Voters have demonstrated they're willing to make additional investments, and as a result, planning is underway to build new parks and preserve additional open space throughout the region.

All of this is not to suggest that Portland has all of the answers. Growth poses many difficult questions that have not yet been answered. For example, how will we ensure a supply of clean water? How will we protect the region's airshed? Where will we find the dollars to build the infrastructure necessary to support a growing economy and manage future growth? What will it take to continue to improve our schools? How will we ensure there is enough affordable housing?

These are tough questions. And while Portland doesn't have all the answers, it does have a proven record of embracing new ideas and daring to do great things. But we also temper our innovation by keeping an eye on the past. Decades of experience trying to build a strong economy and maintain a great quality of life help us make the right choices today.

Portland stands for something special in America. It is a model of innovative planning. It is a place where individuals can still make a difference—and see it in their lifetimes. And it is a community that refuses to rest on its laurels. These characteristics not only make Portland a great place to live and work today, they help make sure it will remain so tomorrow. ∎

Planning is underway to build new parks and preserve additional open space throughout the region.

ONE OF 200 YELLOW LOANER BIKES IN PORTLAND'S INNOVATIVE "SHARE-A-BIKE" PROGRAM. BIKES ARE RIDDEN TO THE BORROWER'S DESTINATION, AND THEN LEFT FOR THE NEXT BORROWER. *PHOTO BY STEVE TERRILL*

QUALITY OF LIFE IS A VALUE PORTLANDERS HAVE LONG SHARED. NEARLY 52.3 PERCENT OF PORTLAND'S RESIDENTIAL TRASH IS RECOVERED, AMONG THE HIGHEST RATES IN THE NATION. RECYCLING—FROM CANS, TO BOTTLES, PLASTICS, YARD DEBRIS, AND NEWSPAPERS—IS A WAY OF LIFE HERE. *PHOTO BY LARRY GEDDIS*

"Group Mackenzie believes that the best is yet to come for Oregon's already dynamic economic environment. Our firm is well on its way toward helping the business community prepare to meet the challenges of future growth. Businesses will look to Group Mackenzie in coming years for creative solutions to constrained site design, sustainable building, transportation systems that work, and structures that maintain the identity of the communities we've helped to build for more than 40 years."

Jeff Reaves
President
Group Mackenzie

BUILT ON EIGHTY-EIGHT
ACRES IN EAST
MULTNOMAH COUNTY,
FAIRVIEW VILLAGE WAS
DEVELOPED AS A
MODEL, PLANNED
COMMUNITY OF SINGLE-
FAMILY HOMES AND
ROWHOUSES. IT ALSO
HAS ITS OWN U.S. POST
OFFICE, CITY HALL,
SCHOOL, AND LIBRARY.
PHOTO BY LARRY GEDDIS

Portland is a product of a visionary citizenry . . .

RIGHT: LAMPPOSTS, DECORATED WITH HANGING FLOWER BASKETS, ARE FOUND THROUGHOUT OLD TOWN, LENDING A NOSTALGIC FEELING TO A PROGRESSIVE COMMUNITY. FAR RIGHT: THE SITE OF PGE PARK HAS BEEN A CENTER FOR OUTDOOR ATHLETIC EVENTS SINCE 1893, WHEN WHAT IS NOW THE MULTNOMAH ATHLETIC CLUB LEASED THIS PLOT OF PASTURE-LAND AND CONSTRUCTED A SMALL GRANDSTAND IN THE NORTHWEST CORNER. HOME TO THE PORTLAND BEAVERS, PGE PARK HOSTS A VARIETY OF OTHER FAMILY-FRIENDLY SPORTS AND ENTERTAINMENT. BOTTOM: YOUNG DOWN-TOWN VISITORS FIND A MOMENT OF RESPITE AT A HISTORIC BENSON BUBBLER. *PHOTOS BY LARRY GEDDIS*

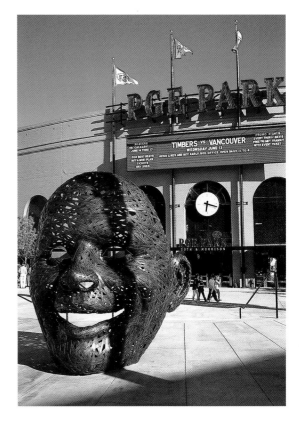

. . . one deeply committed to the notion that few good things happen by accident.

THE 1,200-FOOT FLOATING SECTION OF THE RIVERFRONT ESPLANADE WATERFRONT PARK WALKWAY, A HIGHLIGHT OF THE $32 MILLION PROJECT, TAKES WALKERS AND CYCLISTS ALONG THE WILLAMETTE RIVER, AND BENEATH THE BURNSIDE BRIDGE. OPENED IN 2001, THE ENTIRE MILE-LONG WALKWAY OFFERS SPECTACULAR VIEWS OF THE RIVER AND PORTLAND SKYLINE. *PHOTO BY LARRY GEDDIS*

NEW CONSTRUCTION PROVIDES EMPLOYMENT OPPORTUNITIES AS IT SIGNALS PORTLAND'S CONTINUING GROWTH AS A THRIVING REGIONAL CENTER FOR FINANCE, TRADE, EDUCATION, CULTURE, RETAIL, PROFESSIONAL, AND GOVERNMENTAL SERVICES. *PHOTO BY NICK GARIBBO/ PHOTO DESIGN*

PART

two

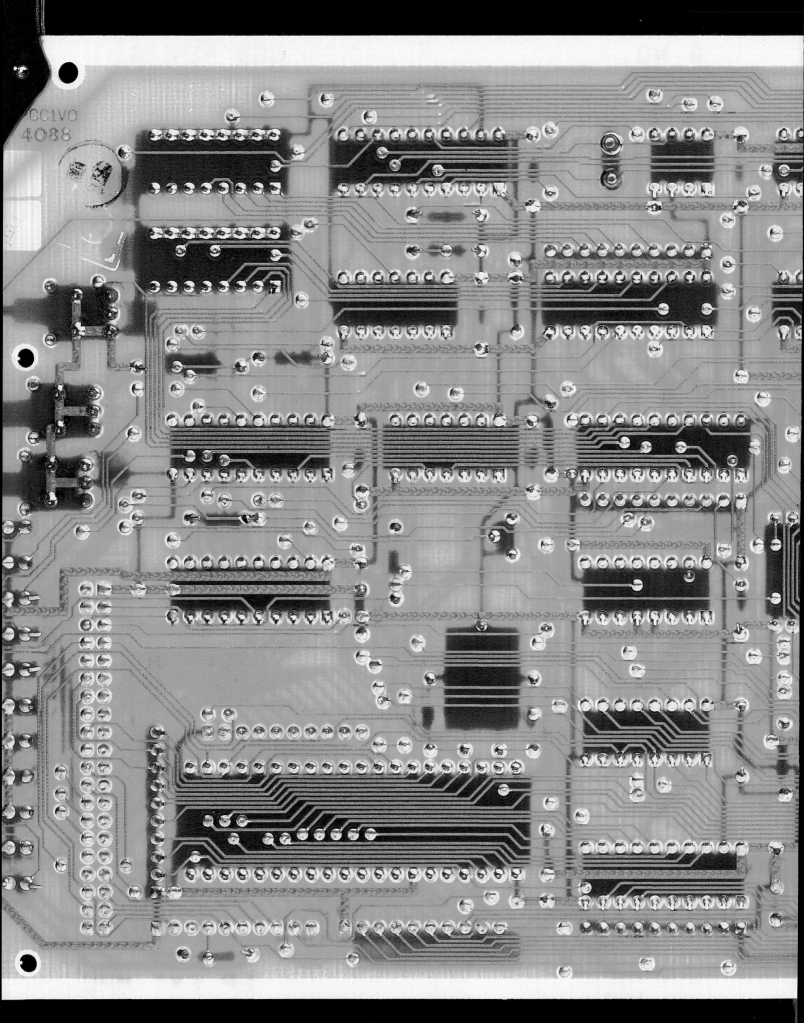

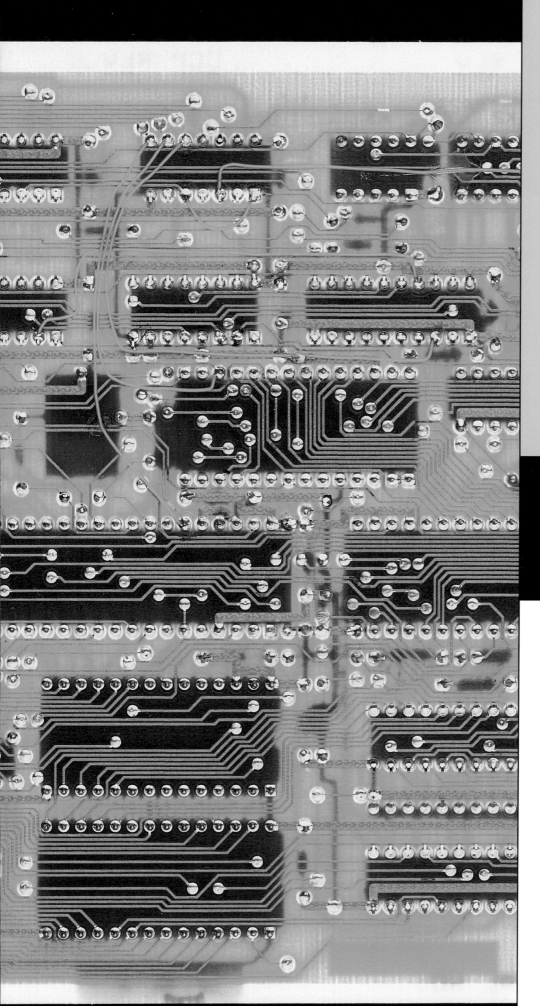

HIGH
TECHNOLOGY

11

PHOTO BY DAVID MCCORD

IDT (INTEGRATED DEVICE TECHNOLOGY)

Celebrating more than two decades of business, with revenues approaching $1 billion for fiscal year 2001, and Integrated Device Technology (IDT) is a leading player in the communications semiconductor world.

Based in Santa Clara, California, IDT's Hillsboro wafer fabrication facility opened for business in 1995 and has helped to establish the Portland-area's growing reputation on the West Coast as the emerging Silicon Forest.

IDT is powering the products that are changing the way people communicate—at work and at home—with products aimed at key sectors of the communications markets. The company is a global semiconductor solutions provider to leading-edge communications companies—those that are driving innovation in the convergence of voice, data and wireless networks.

In Hillsboro, IDT has capitalized on the region's quality of life to attract a highly skilled workforce that is approaching 600. As one of IDT's two wafer fabrication plants, the Hillsboro operation maintains IDT's standards for high quality, cutting edge performance.

IDT's customer list reads like a Who's Who of the communications industry. The company's top 20 customers are among the world's leading communications suppliers—companies such as Cisco, Ericsson, Lucent, NEC, Nokia, and Nortel Networks, to name a few. IDT also works with many of the world's emerging leaders—those companies that are creating next-generation products that will include IDT's leading-edge solutions.

Why do these companies choose IDT? Its high-performance products help accelerate time to market and enhance the performance of systems in emerging data, voice, and wireless networks. IDT has a long history of powering leading-edge, high-performance systems in the communications and computing industries. For more than two decades, IDT has been pushing the technology envelope and has strategically evolved its corporate vision to continually achieve successes.

IDT's Founding Strategy

Right from the start, IDT set out to do something no one had done before with semiconductor process technology, which was the fundamental driver behind nearly all industry innovation at the time. Founded in 1980, the company revolutionized CMOS (complimentary metal-oxide silicon), a fast-evolving process technology that promised to dramatically reduce costs and enable new generations of more highly integrated ICs.

While CMOS was used extensively in products such as calculators and watches, it was an underachiever when it

TODAY, WITH ABOUT 4,000 EMPLOYEES WORLDWIDE SERVING CUSTOMERS IN MORE THAN 40 COUNTRIES, IDT'S CHIPS ARE AT THE HEART OF THE COMMUNICATIONS REVOLUTION.

came to performance. IDT changed all of that by developing the first low-power, high-speed, high-performance CMOS device—an SRAM (static random access memory) with a 90-nanosecond access speed. This technological feat, which literally put IDT on the map, was accomplished just a year after its founding.

With its high-speed CMOS technology, IDT was achieving significant performance breakthroughs. Through 1986, IDT was primarily a supplier of fast SRAMs to every major military prime contractor in the United States. The company also pioneered ICs for up-and-coming technology leaders. From Sun Microsystems' workstations to Silicon Graphics' servers and some of the first high-performance RAID controllers, IDT chips were powering the highest-performing systems at that time.

Without a doubt, the company was establishing a reputation for design leadership and process technology expertise. Yet, the competition was figuring out the secret to fast CMOS technology and many serious players were entering IDT's game.

Memories and More

Recognizing that it had to broaden its offerings to stay competitive, IDT began offering other products such as

logic devices, FIFOs, and dual-port memories. In 1989, IDT strengthened its role as an industry pioneer by entering the RISC microprocessor market as one of the first licensees of the MIPS® architecture. At the same time, CMOS was becoming increasingly mainstream. As a result, CMOS costs were dropping and its uses were expanding well beyond niche applications. The ability to manufacture high-quality parts in commercial volume and price points became a key industry driver. IDT invested significant resources in its manufacturing organization. To complement wafer factories in California, IDT opened its Penang, Malaysia, assembly and test facility in 1988.

During this period, the demand for secondary cache to support powerful new generations of microprocessors exploded. IDT quickly became an industry-leading supplier of SRAMs for the booming PC (personal computer) cache business.

"In the early 1990s, by most measures, IDT was primarily considered a memory company because the lion's share of its products were high-performance SRAMS. That strategy led to tremendous growth for us," explained Jerry Taylor, IDT's president and chief executive officer.

In fiscal 1995, IDT achieved its first $100 million quarter, and in fiscal 1996 the company reported record revenues of $679 million. Life was good in the memory business.

JERRY TAYLOR;
PRESIDENT AND CHIEF
EXECUTIVE OFFICER,
INTEGRATED DEVICE
TECHNOLOGY INC.

Transitioning the Business

In 1995, still in the midst of the SRAM boom and doing exceptionally well in the PC cache business, IDT began taking steps to transition into new areas in anticipation of changing market demands and to improve IDT's long-term viability in the market. Explains Taylor, "We recognized the importance of moving from a cost-driven, cyclical SRAM business to a more value-driven model. And we knew it would become more and more difficult to successfully compete in the commodity memory business."

In 1996 the semiconductor memory market fell dramatically with the price of SRAM plummeting nearly 90 percent by year-end 1996. No company was immune from the impact. Cheap memory chips from overseas suppliers flooded the market. Almost overnight, dozens of companies went from having profitable memory businesses to reporting mounting losses. Margins didn't erode, they evaporated.

Despite those market dynamics, IDT used its SRAM success to reposition and strengthen its traditional businesses and to fund new product and market diversification efforts into new areas. The company saw that its future market growth would come from value-added products offering high performance, differentiated capabilities, and fast time to market. It concentrated on solving problems in the high-speed, high-bandwidth communications market, putting its engineers to work creating new types of communications memories and communication specific products, new approaches to architectural design, and new levels of integration.

Banking on Communications, and Coming Back Strong

In 1997, the company introduced the ZBT® (Zero Bus Turnaround™) architecture, which has become today's de facto standard in new designs with leading networking customers who require the ultimate in system bandwidth. In practical terms, IDT's ZBT architecture can actually double the effective performance of a high-speed switch. IDT now licenses this innovative architecture to partners Micron Technology and Motorola.

IDT also announced its highly integrated two-chip networking product, SwitchStar, a combination memory and controller used in low-cost ATM (asynchronous transfer mode) switches such as DSLAMS. This type of device is typical of IDT's design approach: integrating added functionality (both memory and logic control) onto a single chip.

Before long, the company became the world's leader in communications memories. Led by two broad families of products–FIFOs and dual-ports–communications memories offer clear testimony to the company's leadership claims, delivering the fastest speed, highest density, widest interface, and most extensive set of features. It's why many of the world's leading vendors rely on IDT's parts for their switches, routers, cable modems, cellular base stations, and SONET/ATM multiplexers.

As the communications revolution gained momentum in the mid-to-late 90s, IDT was hard at work delivering a steady stream of innovative, cutting-edge communications products that would enable its customers to add increasing value to the systems they brought to market. To address the needs of the global network, IDT's silicon solutions were targeted at corporate LANS, storage networks, Internet and broadband technologies, and growing wireless networks.

Today, IDT has a broad portfolio of key silicon innovations:
• Communications memories include FIFOS, multi-ports, ZBT, and QDR™ SRAMS;
• Communications ASSPs include ATM switches, TSI/TDM switches, high-speed PHYs and embedded processors;
• High-speed SRAMS; and
• High-performance logic and clock management products.

In March 2000, the company took additional steps to better focus its core competencies on creating whole-product solutions for the communications market–a market forecasted to grow nearly 30 percent each year for the next five years. IDT opened a remote design center near Dallas, Texas, and created the Internetworking Products Division (IPD) to accelerate the development of communications-specific products for the exploding voice, data, and wireless markets.

According to Dave Cúté, vice president of communications ASSPs at IDT, "As the communications market continues to boom, we'll keep refining and evolving our strategy of supplying high-performance, highly featured products to leading-edge communications customers."

To help IDT achieve its goals and enhance its advantages in global markets, IDT has continued to hone its manufacturing strategy. The company's fabrication plants (factories referred to as "fabs" in the business) in California and Oregon, along with assembly and test facilities in Malaysia and the Philippines, give IDT the unique ability to combine functional design with manufacturing strategy–using the right process for the right product. In 2000, IDT reached a major manufacturing milestone by moving its manufacturing facility in Hillsboro, Oregon, to the 0.18-micron process, with anticipation of migrating to .15-micron in late 2001.

This ability, along with a fanatical devotion to quality, has put IDT into an elite group of suppliers on the U.S. military's Qualified Manufacturers List and led to the company receiving the Self-Audit Certification Award–STACK International's highest level of quality compliance. IDT also achieved ISO 14001 certification in fiscal 2000.

The company ended its fiscal 2001 in March, reporting its best revenue numbers to date and growing operating profits dramatically. With revenue of more than $990 million, up 41 percent from 2000, and net income of $3.76 per share. This has been a year of great progress for IDT and its shareholders. They believe the great strides they made are the result of their focus on high-growth Internet and wireless infrastructure segments and on their strong customer-focused business model.

Today, with approximately 4,000 employees worldwide serving customers in more than 40 countries, IDT's chips are at the heart of the communications revolution. ■

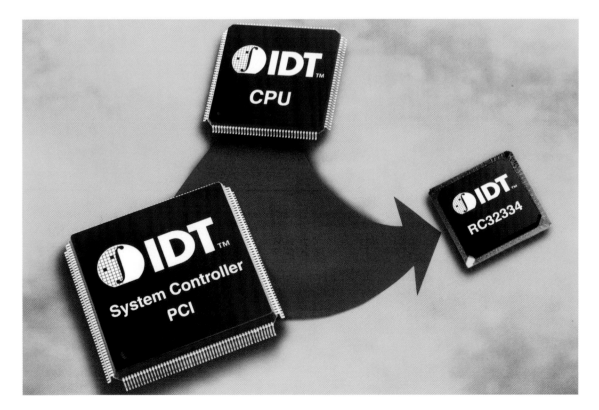

IDT'S FIRST RC32334 INTEGRATED PROCESSOR BASED ON THE RC32300 ARCHITECTURE.

IBM

A visit to IBM's campus in Beaverton, Oregon will help you understand how the global trendsetter in technology is maintaining its leadership in today's fiercely competitive market. Long known for its technological excellence around the world, at Beaverton, the values of IBM are aligned with the values of the Pacific Northwest. This creates an innovative approach to heighten awareness of products that complement other IBM technology offerings.

IBM has enjoyed a notable presence in the state for many years through its sales offices. In 1999, with the purchase of Oregon-based Sequent Computer Systems in Beaverton, IBM established a significant addition to its worldwide network. On the 35-acre Beaverton campus located just west of Portland, more than 1,100 employees produce competitive server products, offer services, sales and technology.

Also close by is the headquarters for the Open Source Development Lab–OSDL–an open source Linux software development group. Founding partners include IBM, and

other leading companies. While not a part of IBM, the organization contributes significant resources to the venture, believing it to be an important resource for the industry at large and a lure for top talent.

Helping employees achieve a balance between personal and professional demands is a key to attracting and retaining the industry's best talent. IBM Beaverton is a place where people work hard to create exciting products for customers.

By supporting a reasonable work/life balance, IBM helps employees shine as effective contributors to their families and the community as well.

Employees are encouraged to use an array of programs such as flexible work schedules, work from home, and wellness programs to keep their lives in balance. In addition to one of the industry's most competitive compensation and benefits packages, IBM Beaverton employees enjoy a wide selection of on-site amenities and discounts through programs such as the "IBM Club" and "Site Swap and Shop." Perks also include on-site concierge service, dry cleaning, massage, and discounted health club memberships. Tri-met bus and light rail passes make getting to work easier. Working parents value the nationally accredited on-site childcare, private kindergarten, and lactation areas for nursing moms. Barbecues and concerts are a part of the summer. Education and Leadership programs are available to

IBM BEAVERTON'S
ON-SITE NATIONALLY
ACCREDITED CHILD CARE
CENTER AND PRIVATE
KINDERGARTEN
PROGRAM GIVES
CHILDREN A QUALITY
ENVIRONMENT AND
THEIR PARENTS A
PIECE OF MIND WHILE
AT WORK.

The Oregon livability is another focus of IBM's civic commitment. SOLV, Stop Oregon Litter and Vandalism, received support from IBM for its recent "Make the Town Clean" campaign. In fact, during the past year more than 50 community activities in Oregon received corporate support of IBM through volunteerism, matching grants programs, technology giving, cash awards, and more.

As an addition to IBM's family of 300,000 employees worldwide, many have asked Beaverton's Senior Location Executive the niche he foresees for the Oregon campus. He states "With the purchase of Sequent we acquired an extremely talented team known throughout the world for innovation. Sequent's skills were a complement to IBM's needs. In addition to high-end server products, we are leveraging skills found here to enhance other IBM missions. This approach creates exciting opportunities in the Portland area as well as bringing new ideas to the rest of IBM." ■

those looking for intellectual challenge. Dependent care resource referrals address the needs of employees caring for children or elderly parents.

IBM's commitment to diversity, which became a stated goal more than 80 years ago when it began to expand internationally, also lends to the dynamic nature of the organization.

Aiming to become the "premier global employer for women," IBM has been recognized as a Top Ten company by *Working Mother* magazine for 14 consecutive years. *Oregon Business Journal* has named it a "Best Company to Work For". *Families in Good Companies* has recognized IBM as the Best Large Company to work for in Oregon since the list's inception.

IndustryWeek magazine named IBM the eighth best managed company in the world. Flexible working hours, and award-winning training programs are among the activities that have received kudos.

Community outreach is a priority for IBM at both the corporate and local levels. A civic focus on education, math, science, and technology creates new opportunities for literally thousands of young people and those entering the workforce each year. In the summer of 2001 IBM hosted technology camps at 22 sites around the world. The Beaverton site was selected and held an EXploring Interests in Technology and Engineering (EXITE) camp which encourages middle school girls to stay excited and involved in math and science. IBM employees also offer the wisdom of their experience through "e-mentoring" programs to show students opportunities that are available to those with strong math and science skills.

FIRST LINUX CLUSTER
SUPER COMPUTER
INTEGRATED AND
SHIPPED FROM THE
BEAVERTON SITE
APRIL 2001.

TRIPWIRE, INC.

W. WYATT STARNES,
TRIPWIRE'S FOUNDER
AND CEO. UNDER
WYATT'S LEADERSHIP,
TRIPWIRE HAS BECOME
ONE OF PORTLAND'S
FASTEST GROWING,
MOST SUCCESSFUL
COMPANIES.

TRIPWIRE, INC. IS THE
LEADING PROVIDER OF
DATA AND NETWORKING
INTEGRITY (DNI)
SOLUTIONS AND
ASSURES THE INTEGRITY
OF INFRASTRUCTURE
IN A NETWORK THAT
CONTAINS "DATA AT
REST." TRIPWIRE SOFT-
WARE IS THE MOST
WIDELY DEPLOYED AND
TRUSTED INTEGRITY
APPLICATION IN THE
WORLD, WITH OVER ONE
MILLION DOWNLOADS
AND A QUARTER MILLION
ACTIVE USERS.

Tripwire, Inc is a Portland-based software development company specializing in data and networking integrity solutions. But more than that, Tripwire—perceived worldwide as a leading player in critical infrastructure monitoring systems—is also one of Oregon's best international business success stories.

Establishing their company in 1997, Tripwire founders Wyatt Starnes, president and CEO, and Gene Kim, chief technology officer, offered an innovative new approach to protecting critical computing systems. Their software product application quickly caught the attention of international corporations at the highest levels. In a relatively short period of time, Tripwire developed an impressive clientele among Global 3000 companies—the world's top tier international businesses. Organizations the caliber of AT&T, the U. S. House of Representatives, and financial firms such as Charles Schwab are among the 1,800 companies that Tripwire now services.

By taking baseline "snapshots" of the system it monitors and then routinely comparing it as the system operates, Tripwire's software is capable of detecting intentional tampering, user error, software failure, as well as the introduction of malicious software or viruses. Rather than working as a perimeter security system, it monitors systems from the inside out—and therein is the simple but brilliant difference that sets the system apart.

The concept was first developed at Purdue University by world-renowned computer security expert Dr. Eugene Spafford and then-student Gene Kim. Purdue chose Tripwire to bring the only commercial version of tripwire software to market.

This is where the Oregon connection emerged. Starnes could have chosen virtually any location to base his company, so why, then, did the 15-year Silicon Valley veteran choose Oregon?

"Quality of life issues," Starnes answers without hesitation, "More room to breathe, less traffic, downtown office space at substantially less cost than the Silicon Valley, and a very high caliber workforce.

"Even though we produce a technology product, we are structured in a very traditional way. We find a higher level of loyalty among employees here and that is more compatible with Tripwire's core values," Starnes added.

Even Tripwire's office space has an air of stability not commonly found among high tech companies. Housed in a remodeled 1920s bank building, the vestiges of that earlier time serve to remind the Tripwire's employees—which now number more than 150—that this is one high tech firm that plans to hold onto the leadership position.

"Oregon values definitely play into our long-term strategy for maintaining the momentum of this company we've created," Starnes commented, " even though we don't actually do much business here. We're well-positioned geographically, as well as financially, and our results will continue to speak for themselves." ∎

PHOTO BY
STEVE TERRILL

12

MANUFACTURING & DISTRIBUTION

PURDY CORPORATION

Consider this: Six out of 10 professional painters in the United States are using handcrafted brushes produced in Portland by the Purdy Corporation. For more than 75 years the company has handcrafted literally hundreds of varieties of world-class, quality painting tools for professionals and the discerning do-it-yourselfer.

The 300-employee workforce at Purdy's Rivergate manufacturing facility turns out an impressive 27,000 paintbrushes per *day*, and as many paint rollers. The painting tools are distributed throughout the United States and internationally to Australia, Canada, New Zealand, and the United Kingdom.

Purdy products are also sold through many of the major home improvement chains such as Home Depot and Lowe's and regional paint manufacturers such as Miller Paint and Rodda Paint. Hardware cooperatives such as Ace and True-Value also carry the Purdy line, as do hundreds of independent paint and hardware retail outlets. Chances are, if you've done any serious painting you've had your hands on a Purdy brush.

An impressive story for a company that had its start in a garage.

Desmond Purdy and his wife began their company with six employees working in a converted two-car garage at the foot of Portland's St. John's Bridge in 1925. In the late 1950's Mrs. Purdy assumed ownership of the still relatively small company, then in 1961 hired David Howard, Sr. to serve as vice president and general manager. Desmond Purdy left a legacy– a superior product–but it was Howard, Sr. who took the company to the next level. Howard who later became president of Purdy and ultimately owner after Mrs. Purdy retired in 1966, used the skills he had learned from a national retail chain to develop a distribution plan for Purdy's products.

Howard envisioned what he called the "feet on the street" strategy–an army of knowledgeable sales people who took the product directly to professionals who would appreciate the fine quality that went into the brushes and rollers.

The strategy worked. During the 1970's sales took off. Howard's two sons, Craig and David E., Jr., joined the company to support their father's efforts. Howard's dream of national distribution was realized.

In 1994 Mr. Howard, Sr. retired and the family chose to sell the company to RAF Industries, an investment group. In 1998 RAF sold to Bessemer Holdings in New York.

PURDY'S CORPORATE WORLD HEADQUARTERS SPAN 100,000 SQUARE FEET AND IS LOCATED IN THE RIVERGATE INDUSTRIAL PARK NEAR THE CONFLUENCE OF THE COLUMBIA AND WILLAMETTE RIVERS.

Howard's son David is still involved with the company as vice president of marketing. Says the junior Howard, "Through four ownerships the one thing that has remained constant is our unwavering dedication to manufacturing hand-crafted tools."

Employees work two shifts at the Purdy plant in the very labor-intensive process of assembling and packaging the product. Purdy Corp. developed and patented many of the exclusive processes they use today. Consequently, it takes six to nine months to train a new brush maker.

Each brush sounds like an individual work of art as proudly described by Howard. The handles are made of Oregon alderwood, "a good lightweight hardwood that compliments the weight of the brush head and gives the tool balance," he explains.

Natural bristles or synthetic fibers, some of which are imported from exotic sources, are carefully measured and weighed and graded by stiffness. Once the bristles are attached, the ends are "chiseled" or shaped at a precise angle. Through the years, Purdy has refined the process using a knowledge of physics that enhances the best possible flow of paint off of the bristles. Every step throughout the process is meticulously inspected, tested, and re-inspected to assure the highest quality of product.

To meet the widely ranging needs of painters, Purdy produces 652 different types of paint brushes and 124 types of roller covers and frames.

The dedication to consistent quality pays off. Howard says the company pursues continuous national advertising, but

that by and large the reputation and performance of the product is spread by word of mouth.

With the heavy investment it makes toward the training of its workforce, Purdy's commitment to the Portland area is a strong one. As a company that understands the importance of team effort, athletic-related pursuits like youth sports, Pee Wee, and Little League baseball are natural civic causes for the company to support. Purdy can frequently be counted on to be among those who donate product for construction-related causes as well.

At a time when many U. S. manufacturing jobs have been lost to foreign countries, the Purdy Corp. demonstrates that quality and pride in product, coupled with listening to the needs of customers, still provides a successful strategy in this age of international competition.

Could Mr. Purdy have foreseen that his product would become an international success three-quarters of a century later? A home improvement magazine recently philosophized that many home improvement buffs achieve an almost Zen-like state of reverie when they wield a paintbrush. For those who have experienced that profound state, it almost makes you wonder if that isn't what led Mr. Purdy to experience his vision for the success of Purdy Corp. ■

PURDY'S UNIQUE HANDCRAFTED MANUFACTURING STEPS, COUPLED WITH UNMATCHED CRAFTS-PEOPLE, CONTINUE TO MAKE PURDY THE NUMBER ONE ASKED-FOR APPLICATOR AND THE CHOICE OF PROFESSIONAL PAINTERS AND DISCRIMINATING HOME DECORATORS WHO DEMAND A PROFESSIONAL-LOOKING JOB.

NIKE, INC.

No company in the history of competitive sport has more successfully captured the essence and passion of athletics than Oregon-based Nike, Inc.

With its world headquarters located in Beaverton, Oregon, Nike markets it products in more than 100 countries. And, whether it's a kid shooting hoops on an asphalt playground or an elite professional or a Monday Night Football fan, anyone who knows sports will tell you Nike is the world's leading sports and fitness company. They are the keepers of the temple ruled by their namesake—Nike, the Greek goddess of victory.

Ever since the day in 1971 when University of Oregon track coach Bill Bowerman poured rubber into his wife's waffle iron in an effort to create a shoe sole that would give his runners a competitive advantage, technological innovation has been the driving force behind Nike's success. Coach Bowerman figured that every ounce he shaved off a miler's shoe would result in 200 fewer pounds lifted over the distance. His lightweight waffle sole became the foundation of Nike—and revolutionized an entire industry.

Nike CEO Phil Knight began his legendary relationship with Bowerman as a runner who had come to University of Oregon to train in the late 1950's. Knight learned from Bowerman that personal excellence and running fast require the same stern stuff. He took those lessons—added the signature Knight vision, attitude, and hard work to the formula—and built a business that today employs more than 20,000 people around the world and creates work for an additional 500,000 whose jobs directly relate to the manufacture of Nike products. Through these activities, Nike plays a major role in promoting economic development with its working partners in Asia and around the world.

The company regularly grosses more than nine billion dollars annually—more than the national product of many countries. Nike has, in fact, created its own country—a global presence that unites its citizens with the passion of a winning team which transcends nationalities.

Knight based his company on several simple philosophies that remain constant. "We are about dreams. We are about the consumer. We are about irreverence. We are about

WITH ITS WORLD HEADQUARTERS LOCATED IN BEAVERTON, OREGON, NIKE MARKETS ITS PRODUCTS IN MORE THAN 100 COUNTRIES.

winning and competing hard." Nike's ability to revolutionize the industry has been driven by a dedication to innovation and a passion to create great product. As Knight puts it, "We make every effort to take consumers where the want to go before they realize they want to go there."

To accomplish its goals Nike has developed a process that requires an extensive cast of sports specialists working in close partnerships with athletes and coaches, conducting in-depth research in the world-class Nike Sports Research Lab, studying and anticipating the marketplace as well as inventing and improving upon cutting edge technology. The process ensures that Nike footwear and apparel directly reflects the specific performance needs of professional and amateur athletes.

As hometown neighbors to its beautiful world headquarters, Oregonians take a special pride in Nike. And it's no wonder. Many here have played a role in Nike's success. And locals appreciate the company's generosity. In Portland and throughout the world Nike gives back to the community with the same passion it markets athletic shoes.

Nike's civic activities range from providing kids with the opportunities and support programs to play sports, to helping people in low income countries with small business start-up capital. Here are just a few of the programs:
• Nike has made a $5 million commitment to the Boys & Girls Club of America to train 40,000 volunteer coaches, triple girls participation in Club activities, and increase overall youth participation in Boys & Girls Clubs by two million kids.
• In the Asia-Pacific region, Nike has launched micro-loan programs in three countries where Nike products are manufactured. The loans are designed to empower people in Nike factory communities to build businesses and spur economic development.
• Nike is investing in the development and education of African American youth through a 3-year, $3 million partnership with the 100 Black Men of America. Nike and 100 Black Men are focusing their efforts on mentoring, education, health and wellness, and economic development.
• Each year, through the Reuse A Shoe program, Nike uses its grind technology to recycle more than two million athletic shoes, using the grind to surface courts such as basketball,

tennis, and playgrounds for under-served neighborhoods. Through the program, Nike has built more than 125 courts in North America alone.

Taken individually, Nike employees are an incredible group of caring individuals. The Nike US Employee Community Involvement Day is just one example of Nike's ongoing employee gift matching program. Twice a year, Nike matches employee' volunteer hours by giving $10 per hour for each hour the employees volunteer at their local non-profit organizations. Nike also matches employee's monetary contributions to qualifying non-profit organizations. Last year, Nike employees donated more than $1.1 million to 745 organizations which Nike matched dollar for dollar.

Through programs like its women's initiative Nike believes that inspiration can also be good business.

As Nike pointed out in a recent annual report, the world now moves faster than most of us could have ever imagined. Nike sees a movement toward a global playground—an intersection where culture mixes with sport to create a new type of athlete. It's a world view that has captured the imagination of millions and leaves little doubt as to whose shoes they use in that new arena of the future. ■

AS HOMETOWN NEIGHBORS TO ITS BEAUTIFUL WORLD HEADQUARTERS, OREGONIANS TAKE A SPECIAL PRIDE IN NIKE.

13

ENERGY &
UTILITIES

PHOTO BY STEVE TERRILL

NW NATURAL

GAS STORAGE IS AN IMPORTANT STRATEGIC COMPONENT FOR NW NATURAL AND PRESENTS BRIGHT OPPORTUNITIES FOR GROWTH IN THE CORE MARKET AND BEYOND. PICTURED RIGHT: AN EMPLOYEE COMPLETES THE TIE-IN OF THE NEWLY DEVELOPED REICHHOLD POOL TO NW NATURAL'S UNDERGROUND NATURAL GAS STORAGE SYSTEM AT MIST.

Just weeks before Oregon officially became a state in 1859, two young men saw the future flickering beyond the candles and kerosene used to light Portland's streets and homes, and began Portland Gas Light Company.

Today, it is NW Natural, and it has expanded its customer base from 49 in less than one square mile to more than 500,000 customers spanning two states. NW Natural's service territory includes the Portland-Vancouver metropolitan area, the Willamette Valley, the northern Oregon coast, and the Columbia River Gorge. The area served by NW Natural is one of the fastest growing regions in the country. In the last 10 years alone, the company's distribution system has grown by more than 200,000 customers.

Over 300,000 Portland households keep warm, cook meals, wash and dry their clothes, and take hot baths with clean, efficient, and cost-effective natural gas. Each day, about 31,000 Portland businesses rely on natural gas for their operations.

FROM PROACTIVE PIPELINE SAFETY TO SYSTEM REPLACEMENT, NW NATURAL LEADS THE WAY IN ENSURING A SAFE AND STABLE TRANSMISSION AND DISTRIBUTION SYSTEM. PICTURED RIGHT: A NW NATURAL CREW REPLACES A CAST IRON PIPE AS PART OF THE COMPANY'S REPLACEMENT OF ITS LOW-PRESSURE DISTRIBUTION SYSTEM.

Where does NW Natural's gas come from? The company originally produced gas by carbonizing coal, which was transported by barge from Vancouver Island in Canada. In 1913, the company built its third (and final) gas manufacturing plant, Gasco. The plant manufactured gas from oil, and the company sold several by-products from this process. Coal briquettes, the principal by-product, were delivered to homes and businesses. In 1955, by-product revenues accounted for roughly one-third of gross company revenue.

The company switched to natural gas in 1936. Natural gas was piped into the company's distribution system though 1,500 miles of pipeline. The pipeline originated in the San Juan Basin in New Mexico and subsequently extended north to Tacoma, Seattle, and the Canadian border.

Today, natural gas is the more preferred energy source for 90 percent of new homes built in NW Natural's service territory, putting the company in a prime position for continued growth. Homeowners choose gas in order to enjoy newer applications of natural gas in the home, such as barbecues, gas fireplaces, gas fireplace inserts, and log sets, along with gas space and water heating.

A strong Oregon economy, bolstered in part by growth of the high-tech industry, contributes to NW Natural's growth. The region's economic growth, which began in Portland, now extends from Clark County, Washington, to Eugene, Oregon, along the I-5 corridor, which is the heart of NW Natural's service territory. Nationally, NW Natural is considered one of the country's fastest growing local distribution companies.

Though the stage is set, NW Natural isn't just waiting for business to roll in. Instead, it is aggressively pursuing market opportunities, and focusing on superior customer service.

As competition increases and the energy industry changes, NW Natural plans to meet consumers' needs in new and expanding ways. Richard Reiten, NW Natural Chairman and CEO, emphasizes that while the company grows, it will continue to stay focused on its natural gas business. "Make no mistake; our core business is, and will continue to be, selling and transporting natural gas as the preferred energy source," Reiten said.

While remaining independent, NW Natural forms strategic alliances with other companies where it makes sense to improve operating efficiencies and customer care. For example, NW Natural and Portland General Electric (PGE) have launched an innovative program called Joint Meter Reading to allow both companies to read meters more efficiently.

Under the program, the two companies have combined some meter reading routes in Portland and Salem. Instead of a PGE employee reading only electric meters at every residence, he or she will also read any natural gas meter on that route. Similarly, NW Natural meter readers will stop at every home on their route to read the PGE electric meters. By coordinating meter reading routes, the two companies will decrease meter reading costs, which will reduce the pressure on gas and electric rates in the future.

Continuing high levels of customer service, ample gas supplies and safe, reliable distribution mean Portland customers can count on NW Natural to provide them with natural gas for decades to come. ■

A MAIN CREW LEADER,

GREG ROOKSTOOL,

WORKING ON A PROJECT

IN ASTORIA, OREGON.

PORTLAND GENERAL ELECTRIC

Portland General Electric has a long history of connecting people, power, and possibilities. It started back in 1889– only 30 years after Oregon became a state–when PGE produced the nation's first long-distance transmission of direct current electricity.

The firm, called the Willamette Falls Electric Company in those days, transmitted power from a generator at Willamette Falls in Oregon City 14 miles downriver to streetlights in Portland. This was just PGE's first step in bringing to Oregonians the possibilities that electricity could provide.

Early Growth

PGE's predecessors also introduced the first electric trolley on the West Coast. The trolley system changed Portland and helped the city grow. As automobiles became popular, the trolley lines began to fade. But household electrical demand was on the rise. PGE not only sold electricity, but also sold electrical appliances. By 1938, electricity moved to the countryside. Demand continued to grow and exploded following World War II.

Today's Safe, Reliable Service

Today, PGE serves nearly 1.5 million people over 3,150 square miles. This area includes 45 percent of Oregon's population and 60 percent of the state's economic base. These residents and business owners use over 19 billion kilowatt hours of electricity each year.

Customers no longer expect trolley rides from PGE. Instead, they simply count on PGE for reliable electric service and innovative energy solutions.

"Our top priority is to make sure our customers have safe, dependable electrical service. That is what we're committed to, every day, just as we have been for more than 100 years," explains Peggy Fowler, PGE's CEO and President.

"In today's turbulent power supply world, we've worked hard and successfully to manage costs and find innovative ways to deliver value to our customers," Fowler said.

Fowler is proud of her company's service commitment. "Whether it's a Web site that makes it easy to do business with us online, a phone system that automatically delivers outage status reports, or our professional customer service staff, PGE strives to deliver value and exceptional customer service," Fowler stated.

To make that promise a reality, the staff at PGE's System Control Center is continuously monitoring and controlling the entire electrical grid, 24 hours a day, 365 days a year, to make sure the power is there when customers need it. PGE's line crews are vigilant about maintaining and repairing their substations and 24,114 miles of transmission and distribution wires.

Besides providing safe, reliable power, PGE is also committed to helping customers use energy wisely and providing them with new energy choices. In the last ten years, PGE's energy efficiency programs have created a virtual power plant powered by electricity customers didn't use. Since 1991, residential and business customers have saved enough energy to power nearly half the homes in Portland.

Along with energy efficiency, innovative power sources like wind and biogas (methane gas created from cow manure), are helping PGE fuel a sound energy future.

Linked to the Community

PGE is recognized for its strong commitment to the communities it serves. Annually, PGE employees volunteer more than 75,000 hours in programs that impacted education, the arts, and environmental/sustainability issues.

PGE contributes funds, expertise, and employee volunteer time to efforts like "One School at a Time" program, which links PGE employees with needs in their local schools. Employees can volunteer in the schools and also nominate schools for grants to help with anything from computer equipment to arts programs or even an area rug where primary students can gather for story time.

As a company deeply rooted in Oregon, PGE is also involved in helping the environment. PGE sponsors Friends of Trees' "Seed the Future" campaign. This campaign, which is aimed at restoring Portland's urban forest, has helped plant more than 144,000 trees and seedlings.

PGE is also a major supporter of Stop Oregon Litter and Vandalism (SOLV), and PGE employees are regular volunteers in SOLV's projects–painting over graffiti, distributing litterbags at the PGE-SOLV Starlight Parade, and cleaning up illegal dumpsites.

In 2000, Portland's former Civic Stadium was renamed PGE Park. PGE's long-term commitment to the landmark will realize its restoration and expansion as a renewed center of civic activity.

For its community service efforts, PGE has received many honors, including the Fair Workplace Project

Leadership Award from Basic Rights Oregon; the 2001 Governor's Arts Award in recognition of outstanding corporate support of the arts; and recognition by Oregon Business Magazine as one of the Best Places to Work in Oregon.

The Future

PGE is well positioned to meet customer needs in the years to come. As the future brings changes and choices, customers can continue to count on PGE to deliver power safely and reliably. PGE will continue to offer innovative energy solutions for customers. And as always, PGE will continue to be actively involved in supporting and improving local communities.

PGE equipment and methods have changed significantly in a hundred years; PGE convictions have not. ∎

VOLUNTEERS HELP PLANT TREES AS PART OF THE FRIENDS OF TREES' "SEED THE FUTURE" CAMPAIGN, WHICH HELPS RESTORE PORTLAND'S "URBAN FOREST."

THIRTY-EIGHT TURBINES ON A WINDY RIDGELINE TRANSFORM WIND CURRENTS INTO ELECTRICITY. BY MAKING A CHOICE FOR CLEAN WIND, PGE CUSTOMERS CAN HELP BUILD A SUSTAINABLE ENERGY FUTURE WITH ADDITIONAL WIND POWER FOR THE PACIFIC NORTHWEST.

BONNEVILLE POWER ADMINISTRATION

A BPA HIGH-VOLTAGE TRANSMISSION TOWER IN EASTERN OREGON IS PART OF A NETWORK THAT DELIVERS ELECTRICITY THROUGH-OUT THE NORTHWEST. BPA'S GRID IS A MAJOR PIECE IN THE WESTERN POWER GRID—AN ELECTRIC HIGHWAY SYSTEM THAT CARRIES POWER FROM CANADA TO MEXICO AND FROM THE ROCKY MOUNTAINS TO THE PACIFIC OCEAN.

The Pacific Northwest is renowned for its scenic treasures–the Cascade Mountain Range, rainforests, the panoramic Pacific coastline, vast deserts, and the inspiring beauty of the Columbia River.

The Columbia and its tributaries define the Pacific Northwest. As the river flows from deep in the Canadian Rockies to the Pacific Ocean, it is fed by rains and melting snows, ensuring the continuous cycle that supplies the lifeblood of the region.

All of this natural splendor also provides one of the most reliable, low-cost power generating systems in the world.

It began in the late 1930s during President Franklin D. Roosevelt's "New Deal" era. A growing need for inexpensive electric power in rural areas of the Pacific Northwest gave birth to one of the most ambitious public works projects in U.S. history, the Federal Columbia River Power System. The goal was to generate low-cost power for rural electrification and regional economic development by harnessing the tremendous hydropower potential of the Columbia River.

In 1937, President Roosevelt signed the Bonneville Project Act, declaring that "the facilities for the generation of electric energy...shall be operated for the benefit of the general public, and particularly of domestic and rural consumers." To carry out this mandate, the act established the Bonneville Power Administration, a federal power-marketing agency headquartered in Portland, OR. Within three decades, the federal government built 29 nonpolluting hydroelectric dams in the Columbia River system.

The result is a reliable, low-cost system that generates nearly half the electricity used in the Pacific Northwest. For more than 60 years, the U.S. Army Corps of Engineers, Bureau of Reclamation and BPA have worked together to manage this extensive hydroelectric system for the benefit of Pacific Northwest residents. BPA built and runs the transmission lines; the Corps and Reclamation built and operate the dams.

Low-cost, nonpolluting hydropower from the Columbia River system has been the driver of the Northwest economy

for more than 60 years and remains a key to the Northwest's economic vitality and quality of life. Any power from the system that is surplus to Northwest needs is made available to neighboring regions.

Rural electrification was just one of several purposes of the region's federal dams. The projects also provide flood control for public safety, irrigation for agricultural development, commercial waterways, and reservoirs for recreation. There was no more dramatic demonstration of the public safety benefits of the system than the Columbia River floods of 1996. River system operations prevented an estimated $3 billion in flood damage in downtown Portland, while keeping the lights on. BPA, the Corps, and Reclamation work together to operate the region's federal hydro system to fulfill all of the dams' multiple purposes for society.

The highest priority in river system operation after public health and safety is protecting indigenous fish and wildlife, especially those listed under the Endangered Species Act. Power production and other functions are carried out within rules set to protect all native species affected by the hydro system and to fulfill mandates for protection and restoration of listed species.

BPA revenues also fund about 300 projects a year to recover and protect fish and wildlife affected by the hydropower system. The projects range from improving hatcheries to repairing spawning streams, researching fish diseases, and controlling predators. BPA works with state and federal agencies and Northwest Indian tribes to manage the most comprehensive fish and wildlife protection effort in the world. It has invested more than $3.5 billion in fish and wildlife protection since 1980.

As the power marketer for this multi-purpose hydro system, BPA was designed to pay its own way without burdening U.S. taxpayers. The U.S. Treasury loaned money needed to construct hydroelectric projects and a massive transmission grid. BPA pays back the money with interest.

CROWN POINT, A VIEW-POINT ON THE OREGON SIDE OF THE COLUMBIA RIVER. BONNEVILLE DAM IN THE BACKGROUND IS A VITAL PART OF THE RIVER'S NAVIGATION NETWORK THAT CARRIES COLUMBIA RIVER BASIN GRAIN TO WORLD MARKETS AND MAKES INLAND PORTLAND A MAJOR SEAPORT.

BPA sells power from the federal dams at cost—it sets power rates high enough to pay for all the costs of producing power, including costs to protect fish and wildlife, encourage energy conservation, and develop renewable resources.

BPA does not operate to make a profit. BPA and the Northwest federal dams are operated for the public good and in the public interest. The Columbia River system provides benefits from the region's dominant natural resource, the Columbia River, to the people who live in the watershed of this Great River of the West.

BPA's nearly 15,000 miles of high-voltage transmission lines knit together the Northwest's power grid across the agency's roughly 300,000 square miles of service territory. From its Vancouver, Wash., control center, BPA's transmission business line schedules and dispatches wholesale power marketed by BPA's power business line and other electric power providers.

BPA lines carry electricity reliably from eastern Montana to Puget Sound, from British Columbia to the California border, and provide three-fourths of the region's high-voltage transmission. Under the 1992 National Energy Policy Act, BPA's transmission business is operated independently of its power marketing function. BPA operates its grid as a common carrier and has provided access to its lines to other utilities since the 1950s.

Like its power rates, BPA's transmission grid is a self-supporting, nonprofit government enterprise. BPA's transmission tariffs are designed to recover all costs of transmitting power and building and maintaining a reliable grid, but not to produce a profit.

BPA is working with other Northwest utilities to create a larger regional transmission organization, RTO West, a nonprofit, nonfederal entity that would serve the entire Northwest and portions of adjoining regions.

The Northwest is well known as a leading region in energy conservation and renewable resource development.

One reason is BPA. In the 1980s BPA pioneered the use of energy conservation to avoid the high cost of building new power plants. In the last two decades, the agency has invested $1.6 billion in energy efficiency, saving enough energy to light Boise and Eugene. Today, BPA offers its power customers incentives to invest in conservation and in new renewable resources, such as wind and geothermal projects. BPA expects to invest as much as $40 million in new conservation and new renewable resource projects each year through 2006.

Working with the independent nonprofit Bonneville Environmental Foundation, BPA also markets green power from certified environmentally preferred resources at a premium price. Revenues from the premiums are plowed back into more green power and fish and wildlife projects in the Northwest. In addition to selling environmentally friendly power, BPA also provides time-of-day pricing, energy management services packaged with power delivery, and custom billing for aggregated services.

In the late 1990s, BPA began installing a fiber optic communications and control network to improve the reliability of its system operations. BPA leases temporarily excess capacity in these fiber optic lines to others, including nonprofit organizations that support rural economic development. This allows rural utilities located along BPA's fiber routes to work with telecommunications companies to extend fiber availability to their communities. Having a high-quality telecommunications link to the world assists in community and economic development.

BPA continues to deliver the clean, low-cost hydropower so vital to the region's economy and quality of life. It delivers the benefits of the federal Columbia River system to the people of the Pacific Northwest. There are many good reasons why people choose to live and work in the Northwest. Regardless of whether you live here or simply visit the region for business or pleasure, BPA will keep the lights on for you. ■

EACH YEAR, SNOWMELT FROM MOUNT HOOD AND OTHER MOUNTAINS OF THE CASCADES AND ROCKY MOUNTAINS PROVIDES THE RENEWABLE FUEL FOR THE NONPOLLUTING ELECTRICITY DISTRIBUTED BY BPA.

GRAND COULEE DAM, LARGEST DAM ON THE COLUMBIA RIVER, PRODUCES AS MUCH ELECTRICITY AS SIX NUCLEAR PLANTS. IT SUPPLIES WATER TO IRRIGATE HALF A MILLION ACRES OF FARMLAND.

PG&E NATIONAL ENERGY GROUP

As the national energy industry evolves—and new entities join the effort to develop and deliver energy resources—one growing force in the Northwest will be familiar: PG&E National Energy Group.

For 40 years, PG&E National Energy group has been an important energy supplier for our region through its natural gas transmission system, PG&E Gas Transmission Northwest (GTN), which is headquartered in Portland.

A METER STATION ON PG&E GAS TRANSMISSION NORTHWEST'S MAINLINE NATURAL GAS PIPELINE SYSTEM IN OREGON. FIRST OPERATIONAL IN 1961, THE PIPELINE TRAVERSES 612 MILES ACROSS IDAHO, OREGON, AND WASHINGTON.

And, since 1995, PG&E National Energy Group has been an owner of the Hermiston Generating Plant, one of the first power plants developed in the region outside of the traditional utility framework.

PG&E National Energy Group, says Sandra McDonough, Vice President, "is at the forefront of an evolving energy industry. We have a keen interest in growing our role as a major energy supplier for the Pacific Northwest. We are in the process of growing our electricity generating assets in the region, and we are expanding our natural gas pipeline system. For the residents of this region, these efforts will mean reliable gas and electric supplies for the long term."

PG&E Gas Transmission Northwest (GTN), incorporated as Pacific Gas Transmission Company in 1957, is one of the largest U. S. transporters of Canadian natural gas. Through their 612-mile, dual-pipeline system, GTN has the ability to ship about 2.7 billion cubic feet of natural gas a day to markets in the Pacific Northwest, Nevada, and California which equates to the energy needs of 12 million households.

IN SERVICE SINCE 1995, THE HERMISTON GENERATING PLANT IS CO-OWNED BY PG&E NATIONAL ENERGY GROUP AND PACIFICORP. THIS NATURAL GAS-FIRED CO-GENERATION PLANT IS CAPABLE OF GENERATING 484 MEGAWATTS OF ELECTRICITY—ENOUGH POWER FOR ALMOST HALF A MILLION HOMES.

GTN's natural gas pipeline begins at the British Columbia-Idaho border and ends at the Oregon-California border, traversing through Idaho, Washington, and Oregon. GTN employs 220 people in the Northwest, with 130 located in Portland.

The Hermiston Generating Plant, which PG&E National Energy Group co-owns with PacifiCorp, is a natural gas-fired co-generation plant capable of generating 484 megawatts of electricity—enough power for almost half a million homes. All of the power from the plant is sold to PacifiCorp. The Hermiston plant employs 27 people.

In its efforts to expand its presence in the Pacific Northwest, PG&E National Energy Group is developing a second power plant across the street from the Hermiston Plant. The Umatilla Generating Project, expected to be operational by late 2003, will be capable of generating 550 megawatts, or enough power for more than half a million homes.

PG&E National Energy Group and PG&E Gas Transmission Northwest are not the same companies as Pacific Gas and Electric Company, the utility, and are not regulated by the California Public Utilities Commission. Customers of Pacific Gas and Electric Company do not have to buy products or services from PG&E National Energy Group or PG&E Gas Transmission Northwest in order to continue to receive quality regulated services from Pacific Gas and Electric Company. ■

PACIFICORP

P acifiCorp does more than provide power–it energizes the communities it serves.

PacifiCorp, a Portland-based electric utility, provides power to 1.5 million electric customers in six Western states as Pacific Power and Utah Power. The company has 8,200 megawatts of generation capacity and supplies electricity to more than half a million Oregon customers.

Formed in 1910 as Pacific Power and Light, PacifiCorp itself was established in 1984 when when its coal mining and telephone businesses grew into full-fledged enterprises. In 1989, PacifiCorp acquired Utah Power and Light Company and, in 1999, it became a part of ScottishPower, a leading utility in the United Kingdom.

PacifiCorp is dedicated to promoting the vitality and economic prosperity of the communities it serves through volunteerism, charitable giving, economic development assistance, energy measures, and other programs that directly touch the lives of its customers and the public.

The PacifiCorp Foundation exemplifies the company's commitment to investing in its communities. Each year, the Foundation provides hundreds of grants to local organizations that promote all facets of learning. The Foundation has awarded nearly $30 million in grants since it was established in 1988.

PacifiCorp and the Foundation are longtime supporters of educational efforts, including Oregon's SMART (Start Making a Reader Today) program, which brings adult volunteers into classrooms, helping more than 10,000 youths improve their reading skills. PacifiCorp also sponsors Rose Festival KIDS, which involves students in local school-based community service projects that range from beautifying neighborhoods to improving local environments. The company has also loaned executives to local groups including Portland's North/Northeast Alliance and Jefferson High School to share business expertise and help nonprofits and schools flourish.

Helping communities is only one aspect of PacifiCorp's commitment to its customers. The company provides a range of efficiency programs to help customers save energy and money, and partners with local agencies to provide weatherization assistance to low-income households. PacifiCorp is also a responsible environmental steward and works hard to minimize the environmental impact of its operations.

PacifiCorp and its employees are dedicated to doing what they do best–continuing a tradition of customer service, affordable power, community support, and environmental protection. ■

14

BUSINESS & FINANCE

PHOTO BY LARRY GEDDIS

PORTLAND METROPOLITAN CHAMBER OF COMMERCE

MAJESTIC MOUNT HOOD TOWERS MORE THAN 11,000 FEET ABOVE PORTLAND'S SKYLINE AND IS THE PERFECT EXPLANATION POINT FOR THE REGION'S BEAUTY. *PHOTO BY STEVE TERRILL*

I f time is the best judge of quality, then the livability and economic vibrancy of Portland, Oregon is testimony to the work of the Portland Metropolitan Chamber of Commerce. Fueled by the energy and expertise of its 1,800 member companies, the Chamber has been a catalyst for positive growth and business prosperity in the region since 1890.

The Portland Chamber is the region's leading business association and ranks among the eight largest Chambers on the West Coast of the United States. Its member companies reflect the diverse economic base of the region and are responsible for providing more than 300,000 jobs in the area. Almost 85 percent of the Chamber's members are small businesses with 50 or fewer employees—a statistic that reflects Oregon's positive climate for business development.

The Chamber's objectives are two-fold: to create a favorable business climate today and for the future and to promote the growth of its member companies through a well-balanced combination of networking opportunities, education, information, and public policy advocacy.

RESIDENTS DON'T HAVE TO GO FAR TO FIND A GOOD CAMPING SPOT. IN FACT, MANY CHOOSE THE BANKS OF THE WILLAMETTE JUST SOUTH OF THE DOWN-TOWN CORE AREA FOR THEIR WEEKEND GET AWAYS. *PHOTO BY STEVE TERRILL*

In the past decade, Oregon's economy has changed from one that relies heavily on natural resources and agriculture to one that draws much of its momentum from the knowledge-based technology industry. Despite this fundamental shift, many of the issues addressed by the Chamber today are surprisingly similar to those that prompted business leaders to come together and create the association more than 100 years ago. The solutions are far more complex, however.

Education is a good example. A hundred years ago, the Chamber worked with community leaders to build schools. Today the continued success of Oregon's new economy depends on the ready availability of workers with leading edge skills. To meet this challenge, the Chamber is collaborating with Portland public schools, elected public officials, concerned parents, and the business community to establish stable funding sources for an education system that will provide a well-trained and qualified workforce. The education strategy includes a strong school-to-work component to meet the increasing need for skilled and technical workers. The Chamber is also supporting other public and private entities working to develop innovative higher education programs that focus on new-economy skills.

Transportation is another common theme the Chamber has championed throughout its history. Then as now, the Chamber's leaders have recognized that a well-planned transportation system is essential for linking the region's businesses with domestic and international markets. In the 1800s, the Chamber advocated for building the state's first roads and deepening the Columbia River to establish Portland as center of commerce on the West Coast.

As Portland has emerged as an international gateway for Pacific Rim trade, the growth in opportunities has put

tremendous pressure on the existing systems of roads, bridges, and mass transit, and created new demands for air and ocean-borne transportation options. The Chamber is working with the region's leaders to develop a cost-effective transportation strategy that addresses the region's needs for moving people and freight. The Chamber has joined with others who have identified deepening the Willamette and Columbia River channels and transportation funding for roads and mass transit as the region's priority issues.

Building bridges of another sort is yet one more critical role of the Chamber. The fast-paced change in today's markets makes it essential that all factions within the state work together to insure a positive climate for continued economic growth. The Chamber is working with other chambers throughout Oregon to find common ground on issues of mutual concern. The alliances forged by the Chamber have helped to create a broad base of support in the state legislature for issues important to the business community. The collective voice has also provided the leadership necessary to keep down the cost of government. Since the early 1990s, businesses have been spared millions of dollars of increased taxes thanks to the intervention of the Portland Chamber.

The region's livability provides a strong competitive advantage for keeping and attracting the best employers

and workers. Recognizing this, the Portland Chamber takes an active role in addressing social issues that affect the quality of life for all Oregonians.

Even before the listing of endangered salmon, the Chamber closely monitored the recovery plans developed by local and state officials to make sure that natural habitats along the Columbia and Willamette rivers would be improved and restored in a manner that would not unfairly target area businesses.

The Chamber's affiliate, the Citizens Crime Commission, is working to address the root issues of crime with the goal of maintaining the metropolitan area's reputation as a safe community. The Chamber's newest affiliate, the Oregon Mentoring Initiative, works to connect adult volunteers with high quality mentoring programs serving young people who need adult support and guidance. The list goes on and on.

The Chamber also recognizes how important it is for members to develop networks and cultivate contacts. Throughout the year, the organization offers well-attended programs and events that allow interaction with the region's business leaders. Personal and professional development opportunities allow employers to keep up to date on issues, marketing, and management practices. The Chamber also serves as an information resource, providing members with a Web site—www.pdxchamber.org—and a wide assortment of informational publications, data bases, and directories.

In general, you might say the business of the Portland Chamber is to provide leadership and vision. And for more than a hundred years, business has been very good! ■

STREET SIGNS IN PORTLAND'S HISTORIC "OLD TOWN/CHINATOWN" ARE IN ENGLISH AND CHINESE. POPULAR WITH TOURISTS AND LOCAL CITIZENS ALIKE, THIS AREA IS PLANTED WITH COLORFUL SPRING-BLOOMING TREES. *PHOTO BY STEVE TERRILL*

OFTEN CALLED THE CITY OF BRIDGES, THE ST. JOHN'S BRIDGE IS ONE IF 11 IN PORTLAND THAT CARRIES TRAFFIC ACROSS THE WILLAMETTE RIVER. *PHOTO BY STEVE TERRILL*

U.S. TRUST

As one of the nation's oldest trust and investment companies, U.S. Trust provides comprehensive wealth management services to individuals, families, foundations, non-profit organizations, and corporations. The professionals of U.S. Trust understand that significant wealth is not the end of worry, it is the beginning.

Founded in 1853, U.S. Trust manages assets in excess of $90 billion nationally and more than $10 billion on the West Coast. The Portland office, which includes 60 employees, was established in 1993 through the acquisition of Capital Trust Co. Headquartered in New York City, U.S. Trust has offices located in California, Connecticut, Delaware, Florida, Minnesota, New Jersey, New York, North Carolina, Pennsylvania, Texas, Virginia, and Washington, D.C.

Through a combination of investment management, fiduciary, and private banking services, U.S. Trust offers a comprehensive and personal relationship approach for clients with an account minimum of $2 million. The firm begins with a proven, tax-intelligent investment process. U.S. Trust offers numerous investment options, including domestic and international equities, taxable and tax-exempt fixed income, and alternative investments including private equity, hedge funds, and real estate. Over the years, U.S. Trust has compiled an enviable long-term record of investment performance, out-performing the major indices and many competitors in both equity and fixed-income investing on both a pre-tax and after-tax basis.

But the guidance of U.S. Trust goes far beyond investment strategies. In addition, the firm provides an array of sophisticated, value-added services including financial consulting, inter-generational wealth transfer options, foundation management and philanthropic giving strategies, strategic trading, and risk management consultation involving both assets and liabilities.

Education is an important component of the service the company provides its clients. Individual consultations and seminars provide clients and their families information to assist them in making informed financial decisions.

U.S. Trust employees are experienced and well versed in the legal, financial, and tax needs unique to wealthy families. The professional staff includes individuals with successful backgrounds in investment management, banking, accounting, law, and related fields. The firm is also well networked with local and national estate planning attorneys, tax consultants, high-end life insurance professionals, and others that can provide sound advice tailored to the individual circumstances of each client.

U.S. Trust's advisors make it their job to stay in close contact with clients to keep abreast of any changes in their circumstances that may require attention. Likewise, the firm conducts ongoing proprietary investment research to identify new financial opportunities as they become available. The goal is to anticipate needs and address them before the client needs help. U.S. Trust simplifies clients' financial affairs, so they can focus on the most satisfying aspects of life. ■ *Non-deposit investment products are not FDIC-insured or bank guaranteed and are subject to investment risk, including possible loss of principal. Member FDIC. Equal Housing Lender.*

THE WILLIAM C. EARHART COMPANY, INC.

PORTLAND OFFICE STAFF.

Combining personal service and efficiency is the unique formula that spells success for the William C. Earhart Company, Inc.

An employee benefits administrator that has served the Northwest since 1960, the company headed by founder Bill Earhart, has evolved into a family operation guided by a partnership that includes President and CEO Hannah E. Sutton and Vice President Catherine Gladstone–Earhart's daughters.

It is perhaps that "family touch" that sets the company apart in an industry that deals with people at some of their most frustrating times.

Says Earhart, "We administer all types of employee benefit plans including pensions, health plans, apprentice programs, flexible spending accounts, medical reimbursement programs, and multi-employer trusts. We do business nationally with a strong focus in the Northwest including Oregon, Washington, Idaho, Montana, and Alaska."

"We provide administrative services for single employers as well as jointly trusteed Taft-Hartley or multi-employer plans. The plans may include as few as 20 participants or as many as 20,000," Earhart said.

"But regardless of the size," he emphasized, "we care about the participants. We treat everyone who calls in like they're family. Every explanation of benefits goes out with the name and phone number of one person who becomes that client's advocate. Real people answer phones here. Because we are a family-based organization we have a long-term stake in making our business succeed. Consequently, we have low turnover of employees. Our clients benefit from our employees' experience and the situation builds pride."

Today the Earhart Co. includes a staff of 56 professional employees who work at three offices–two in Portland and the third in Salem, Oregon.

During the past 40 years, Earhart has witnessed the evolution of a system that has become increasingly complex and regulations which have undergone monumental change. Earhart, Sutton, and Gladstone understand their role is to reduce the oftentimes consuming myriad of details that confront plan sponsors, employers, and employees.

The company has responded to the increasing complexity by taking what Earhart calls "an old fashioned approach of taking time with people" and then combining that with a depth of industry knowledge supported by the most sophisticated data and electronic systems. They stay abreast of the latest information by actively participating in the industry's leading educational organizations. Earhart and Sutton have served as directors of the International Foundation of Employee Benefit Plans and are the first father-daughter duo to earn the Certified Employee Benefit Specialist designation awarded by that organization and The Wharton School of Business, University of Pennsylvania.

When asked if there is any one secret to the success of his company, Earhart sums it up like this, "If you enjoy what you're doing, pride in doing it well is automatic, if you don't enjoy what you're doing it's time to move on." ∎

SALEM OFFICE STAFF.

BECKER CAPITAL MANAGEMENT

An interweaving of business and community values is at the heart of Becker Capital Management's value-based approach to investment strategy. It is this commitment that has spelled success for the firm, its clients, and the community.

Patrick E. Becker, the company's founder explains, "Throughout our 25 years of service we have demonstrated an unwavering commitment to value investment. We take a long-term approach—with rewards based on a sound long-term strategy rather than trends."

Today Becker manages approximately $2 billion in total assets for about 200 clients. Approximately 70 percent of the asset base is managed equity portfolios and the remainder is balanced accounts.

Pat founded Becker Capital Management in 1976, following nine years experience with a nationally recognized brokerage firm, where he specialized in advising high-net-worth individuals. Building on his knowledge of the special needs of the affluent, the company built its reputation in the 1970s and 1980s growing the assets of clients with a million dollars or more to invest.

Janeen McAninch, president and chief operations officer, with the firm since 1987 adds, "Our efforts to personalize service, combined with our long term performance have resulted in relationships that are literally passed down through generations—we are now investing for the sons and daughters of our clients. That depth of personal knowledge helps us to anticipate needs, educate our clients, and help them set realistic strategies and goals."

In the 1990s Becker's successful value-oriented investment style attracted an additional base of institutional clients from around the United States.

Says Michael Malone, Becker's senior vice president of investments, "In our first 15 years we established a tremendous base of service and a sound investment style philosophy. It was a natural extension to expand to clients in the national market."

Since that time, the firm has gained a national reputation and handles the needs of clients from coast to coast. About 60 percent of the firm's investors are now institutional, including corporations, endowments, foundations, union trusts, and public funds.

To handle investment research, asset management, and client services, the firm has grown to include 25 employees, including 17 investment professionals. The dynamic nature of the firm is preserved in an atmosphere where both the young and experienced alike share in the ownership and direction of the company.

Becker is proud of his colleagues' civic involvement, and sees personal commitment to the community in harmony with the firm's professional goals. Because as Pat explains, "Becker Capital Management understands that preserving and growing capital allows clients to apply assets for good purposes." ■

TRANSFAC

TRANSFAC is a Portland-based company that for almost 60 years has helped businesses maintain financial health by providing a very specialized tool called "factoring." Simply put, factoring involves the purchase of a company's accounts receivable for immediate cash. TRANSFAC "buys" the company's outstanding invoices, pays the company for them

immediately, and then assumes responsibility for collection of the receivables. Not only does the company have quicker access to its money, but outsourcing the billing department function frequently creates an operational cost savings. The company is, in turn, able to dedicate its resources to more profitable activities. For performing this service, TRANSFAC charges a small percentage of the overall receivables.

TRANSFAC is one of Portland's largest factoring companies and one of the longest established nationally. It grew out of a Northwest trucking cooperative, which started almost 60 years ago. Interstate Commerce regulations of the day required that the truckers' billing and collections occur within seven days and at regulated rates. Transportation companies banded together to create a company that would take over that sometimes daunting function. Today, transportation still constitutes a large share of TRANFAC's business, but companies from a variety of industries are finding that factoring results in a number of advantages for them as well as more consistent and dependable cash flow, reduced credit risk, better reporting systems, and lower overhead.

In addition to collections, TRANSFAC monitors the financial health of a company's vendors. Experience in this very specialized area and the ability to recognize "red flags," enables TRANSFAC to anticipate potential payment problems and work with vendors.

Since money is the lifeblood of business, it is understandable that TRANSFAC treats its relationship with

clients very carefully. Long-term retention of clients is one of TRANSFAC's major goals and in an industry where 18 months is the standard, TRANSFAC's average relationship with clients is more than 10 years–some client's have depended on TRANSFAC for more than 30 years. That longevity speaks to the quality of the company that chooses TRANSFAC.

From its inception, TRANSFAC has been structured to allow greater flexibility than most financial institutions. Since TRANSFAC assumes a long-term relationship with each client, a great deal of thought goes into developing their process to fit the need of the customers. It's a customer service concept that is more than just words. One client may be a trucking firm generating 1,200 to 1,500 invoices a month or it may be the specialty toy manufacturer who works out of a garage–each feels that TRANSFAC is just right. And, each is equally right for TRANSFAC.

They say that the most successful companies are the ones built around the simplest ideas. What could be a better example of that truism than TRANSFAC? Ask any businessperson: Would you rather be waiting for your money or working with it? ∎

CENTENNIAL BANK

CENTENNIAL BANK MAKES THE BENJAMIN FRANKLIN PLAZA BUILDING IN DOWNTOWN PORTLAND ITS CORPORATE OFFICE HEADQUARTERS.

Centennial Bank is an independent, locally owned and managed full-service bank. Since 1999, Centennial Bancorp and Centennial Bank have had their headquarters in the Portland downtown business district. Centennial Bank is currently the second largest, publicly traded Oregon-based bank, serving customers from more than 20 branch locations along the I-5 corridor between Vancouver, Washington, and Cottage Grove.

The bank also operates seven Commercial Banking Centers to provide relationship-based financial services to middle-market business clients. Centennial's real estate finance division—Centennial Mortgage—has five offices based in Portland, Salem and Eugene. Centennial Bank also caters to retirees in a big way, managing seven part-time branches in Portland area retirement centers.

Whatever the venue, Centennial emphasizes superior customer service at every level to commercial and industrial clients, business enterprises, public entities, professionals executives, and individuals. The bank provides customers with a broad suite of business and consumer financial products, including new offerings such as CB-Onlinebanking and Merchant Banking. Centennial Mortgage complements the bank with a full range of residential and commercial mortgage lending products.

THE BANK'S ADMINISTRATIVE CENTER IS LOCATED IN DOWNTOWN EUGENE.

Centennial Bancorp has demonstrated an impressive financial track record since it was established in 1981, ranking among the most profitable banking organizations in the western region of the country. As of March 31, 2001, the bank's assets stood at $857 million, more than double since 1996. Deposits increased in 2000 by 22 percent over the prior year; loans grew 19 percent.

Centennial's success is due, in part, to its unique approach with business clients. Centennial's experienced executive management team, headed by 30-year industry veteran President and Chief Executive Officer Ted R. Winnowski, places a special emphasis on "high touch and right touch" personal service. Not unlike the days when doctors made house calls, Centennial's highly motivated and seasoned bank officers from the top down frequently call directly on the businesses they serve. This direct, personalized approach facilitates a true understanding of customer needs to tailor right-fitting and integrated financial service solutions.

The ever-increasing list of offerings includes professional accounts, executive accounts, ultra rate fund accounts, cash management services, merchant banking, merchant bankcard services, and tiered money market accounts. Increasingly, Centennial is partnering with other companies to provide customers with even more product options. Its flexible equipment leasing program for businesses, for example, is offered through Textron Financial Corporation, a well-recognized, national company.

"We believe our success rests with our ability to understand our customers' needs and support their success," Winnowski said.

Centennial Bank's commitment to the community extends well beyond business and personal banking service to the most personal level. Since many of organization's employees have lived and worked in their respective communities for years, they are well known figures with strong attachments to community activities. Officers make significant contributions through regular civic involvement and participation.

CEO Winnowski points with pride to these employees when he says, "Our exceptional employees characterize our mission: we persistently strive for excellence and superior performance in our organization. At Centennial Bank we are always "Open for business—everywhere we do business!" ■ *Member FDIC. Equal Housing Lender.*

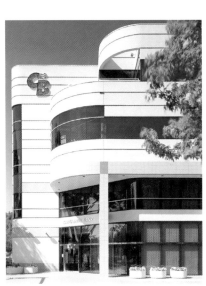

WEST COAST BANK

In today's financial marketplace, West Coast Bank's proud Oregon heritage sets it apart. The West Coast Bank story began in 1925 when it first opened its doors under the Bank of Newport name, on the historic Newport, Oregon bay front.

Since then, West Coast Bancorp, now with corporate offices in Lake Oswego, Oregon, has grown to become the largest publicly traded bank holding company headquartered in Oregon. West Coast Bancorp serves as the parent company for West Coast Bank and West Coast Trust.

As Oregon's local bank, West Coast Bank has retained the core values which have guided the company since it was founded–integrity, exceptional customer service, and local decision-making. Backed today by $1.4 billion in assets, West Coast Bank is a strong and stable institution with best-of-class products and services made available to customers at more than 40 convenient branch locations, including the first bank opened in Newport more than 75 years ago.

West Coast Bank continually repositions itself to meet the changing needs of the business community. A full menu of easy and flexible programs designed for managing business finances helps clients respond to today's fast-paced business environment.

WEST COAST BANK IS THE LARGEST PUBLICLY TRADED BANK HOLDING COMPANY HEADQUARTERED IN OREGON.

Specially designed business banking solutions include a sophisticated Internet-based Treasury Management product suite, specialized commercial loan centers, comprehensive merchant card services, business investment management services, and equipment leasing options.

Competitive rates and terms are available on construction funding for new projects of any size. Acquisition and subdivision development loans, loans for speculative projects, construction-only loans, and even an all-in-one loan combining the construction and permanent loans are all approved close-to-home, allowing for quick turn-around during construction. This same local control eases tight timetables for inspections, requested advances and disbursement of loan funds.

Local West Coast Trust investment professionals are experienced in asset management and adhere to a proven investment strategy that has consistently produced superior returns.

PrimeVest investment representatives at West Coast Bank offer a full range of services to help business owners achieve their goals–money market funds, life insurance, stocks and bonds, mutual funds, tax-advantaged products, retirement plans, and 401(k) plans.

For those who prefer the convenience of 24-hour self-service banking, easy options are available by phone, personal computer, and ATMs. Clients can pay bills, transfer funds, or make loan advances and payments on West Coast Bank's user-friendly web site.

A financial solution provider for every financial need–that's what West Coast Bank has become. But in every business transaction, the signature customer service that has defined the company through the years remains the rock-solid foundation. Oregonians can count on West Coast bank for caring, local professionals involved in their communities, serving their neighbors, and helping them succeed. ■ *Member FDIC.*

WEST COAST BANK CONTINUALLY REPOSITIONS ITSELF TO MEET THE CHANGING NEEDS OF THE BUSINESS COMMUNITY.

15

THE PROFESSIONS

SRG PARTNERSHIP, PC

Time and again, one Portland architectural firm has demonstrated a talent for recognizing the essential elements that define our West Coast culture and successfully translating those elements into man-made structures that have become landmarks for the region, its inhabitants and its institutions.

SRG Partnership, PC–founded in 1972–is one of Oregon's leading architectural, planning, and interior design firms. Through the years the firm has demonstrated the ability to imaginatively apply knowledge and experience to create successful design solutions for a wide range of projects, including many of the region's largest and most notable public facilities.

Interestingly, SRG projects are noted for creating "client signature" pieces rather than designs driven by the architect's personal style. Common principles, which have consistently guided the firm's approach to design, assure that structures will physically embody the values of the client for whom they design and result in buildings that will make a lasting contribution to their communities.

"What sets us apart from our competitors is our approach to working with clients," explains SRG Partnership's principal architect for design Jon Schleuning, FAIA. "We spend more time listening to them, especially at the beginning of the process, to develop a clear understanding of our client's business, culture, aspirations, and needs. This is important because the majority of our clients are owners and users; they will be living in the buildings we create for the next 40 years."

One SRG effort, the award-winning Oregon Coast Aquarium, has become an Oregon Coast destination for millions of visitors. SRG maintained its 13-year relationship with the Aquarium throughout the design of the "Passages of the Deep" exhibit, which transformed the former home of the whale Keiko into a dramatic underwater interpretive exhibit.

The Oregon Market retail stores at Portland International Airport created in partnership with the Port of Portland establishes the first memorable impressions of Oregon for millions of domestic and international travelers each year.

GENENTECH, INC. FOUNDERS RESEARCH CENTER I (PHASE II UNDER CONSTRUCTION), SAN FRANCISCO, CALIFORNIA: THE WORLD'S LARGEST BIOTECHNOLOGY RESEARCH COMPLEX UPON COMPLETION.

PHOTO BY DOUGLAS KAHN

The Mount St. Helen's Visitor Center in Southwest Washington is another SRG undertaking that captures and enhances the sense of beauty and the awesome forces of nature to be found in the Pacific Northwest.

SRG has also become a respected leader in the planning and design of academic facilities throughout the West Coast. More than 20 college campuses in Oregon, Washington, Idaho, and California have selected SRG to meet diverse needs. SRG's academic portfolio is impressive: the design of research and instructional facilities for the School of Veterinary Medicine at the University of California at Davis; a major expansion and modernization of the University of Oregon's historic Museum of Art; leading-edge teaching and support spaces for the Lundquist College of Business at the University of Oregon; The Valley Library and College of Forestry at Oregon State University; and design of research laboratories which will support the most advanced biomolecular, physiological, and behavioral science research at the Oregon Health & Science University.

"Our clients can give us an historic and geographic context for the project and guide us in our search for the ideals that reflect their institution. We encourage activities such as touring other facilities together and visioning workshops help to create a common vocabulary, which enables us to

TOP: THE VALLEY LIBRARY, OREGON STATE UNIVERSITY: 1999 AMERICAN LIBRARY ASSOCIATION LIBRARY OF THE YEAR; IN ASSOCIATION WITH SASAKI ASSOCIATES. *PHOTO BY GREG HURSLEY*
LEFT: FOREST ECOSYSTEM RESEARCH LABORATORY, OREGON STATE UNIVERSITY; NATION'S LEADING FORESTRY SCHOOL. *PHOTO BY GREG HURSLEY AND GARY TARLETON*

PORTLAND
INTERNATIONAL
AIRPORT, RETAIL
CONCESSIONS,
PORTLAND, OREGON:
NATIONAL MODEL FOR
AIRPORT RETAIL.
*PHOTO BY
ED HERSHBERGER*

better explore alternatives and options in design charettes. We pose the question: If you were to build your culture— what would it look like? What material or feature or shape would embody your ideals? How could the structure itself support the success of your endeavor?"

"We are very good at taking the information and reapplying SRG's 30 years of knowledge and experience in a way that is fresh and innovative. The dynamic of the relationship becomes an integral part of the design process. We challenge the client and the client challenges us," Principal Dennis Cusack explains.

"Our goal is to understand our client's business and help them reach their strategic objectives. We measure our success by our ability to understand the client's needs at multiple levels and to develop solutions that maximize the value of the organization both qualitatively and quantitatively," says Roz Estimé, Principal.

With a clientele that includes university administrators, managers and CEO's of the most sophisticated biotech firms, and high visibility public administrators, a trusting relationship that enables creative exploration must be balanced by a strictly disciplined, detail oriented and hard-nosed approach to project programming, budget and schedule. "We've demonstrated our respect for the responsibilities of the $120 million project," points out Schleuning.

Part of SRG's formula for creative success is found in the diversity of its associates. The 75-member firm is led by Principals Jon Schleuning, FAIA; Dennis Cusack, AIA; Roz Estimé; Laura Hill, IIDA; Kent Duffy, AIA, (President of the AIA Portland); John Harrison, AIA; Kenneth Mouchka, AIA; Skip Stanaway, AIA prides itself on its wide range of areas of expertise, and dynamic mix of age, gender, and ethnicity. "The staff is culturally varied, and bridges wide professional and educational backgrounds.

VETERINARY MEDICINE
LABORATORY AND
INSTRUCTIONAL
FACILITY, UC DAVIS,
SCHOOL OF VETERINARY
MEDICINE: TOP-RANKED
VETERINARY MEDICINE
PROGRAM IN
NORTH AMERICA.

As a firm, we are well traveled, committed to research, and bring an open mind and broad perspective to our work," says Principal Laura Hill. "This allows the firm to be more sensitive to the ideals of clients, and more aware of the evolving roles of the design professional."

"The collaborative process of design has changed dramatically, and expectations have broadened. It is not unusual for our firm to become an advocate for project funding as one example," says Principal Dennis Cusack, says pointing to SRG's role with the fundraising campaign for Lillis Business Complex at the University of Oregon.

New standards for sustainable design, a resurgent appreciation of fine craftsmanship, and the ever-increasing use of technology as a design aid all contribute to the shifting picture of design.

But for SRG, one factor remains constant: The joy and excitement that comes from exploring unique challenges and discovering creative solutions. Says Schleuning, "We will always continue to strive for imaginative, insightful, and refreshing designs that reveal the fundamental character of each project. At SRG, we have a faith in the future and a commitment to help shape it." ■

TOP: LILLIS BUSINESS COMPLEX, UNIVERSITY OF OREGON: FIFTY-PERCENT MORE EFFICIENT THAN THE CURRENT ENERGY CODE REQUIREMENTS. LEFT: OREGON COAST AQUARIUM, NEWPORT, OREGON: INTERNATIONAL DESIGN AWARD WINNER. *PHOTO BY RICK KEATING*

OFFICE SUITES AND SERVICES

OUTSTANDING VIEW
OF THE PORTLAND
WESTERN HILLS.

Business and legal professionals seeking convenient, downtown office space supported by a full complement of business services need look no further than Office Suites and Services.

Office Suites features seven tastefully appointed executive suites, meeting, and conference rooms which provide a personal yet professional work environment. Friendly, experienced staff and a resident computer consultant assure that the details of office management are handled smoothly and efficiently. Telephone reception, word processing, fax capabilities, database set-up and maintenance, mailing services, drop-in computer stations, data ports, and Internet teleconferencing transcription are among the services provided.

In addition, Office Suites and Services features specialized support to meet the needs of legal professionals, including legal secretarial and transcription services. Close proximity to county and federal courthouses provides a winning combination for attorneys—either as a main office or a downtown satellite for suburban firms.

Gary Miller, owner, says that his clientele also includes a cross-section of other professionals from doctors to marketing consultants to real estate brokers. "Our first objective is to provide personal, high quality service to our clients, regardless of their profession or needs," Miller stated.

Shelli Kennedy, office manager, points out that Office Suites also provides a "virtual office" location for home-based business owners seeking telephone reception, secretarial services, legal mailing address, and "drop-in" work and meeting spaces. "We can actually handle home-based client calls exactly as if those clients were in our facility," she added.

Gary believes that improvements in technology will continue to expand the opportunities for home-based businesses, and he works to serve as an up-to-date information source on the practical applications of technology. But he hastens to add that, "Nothing will ever replace face-to-face quality service; technology can only improve the timeliness and accuracy of our services."

Gary realized his dream of becoming a small business owner in 1999 when he purchased and built upon the 33-year history of the Dorothy Bays Secretarial Service. An electrical engineer by training, and later a technology sales and marketing professional, Gary had traveled the nation extensively as a high tech marketing consultant. His previous experience has benefited his present clients in two ways: having experienced the best and the worst of drop-in office services during his time on the road, he understands customer service needs first-hand; and secondly, his technology expertise enables him in assisting clients to "bridge their technology gaps". (Gary also manages a computer consulting business that focuses on the networking needs of small businesses.)

Gary emphasizes that the most important quality he brings to his clients is a can-do attitude. "My competitive advantage is that we always say 'yes' when others say 'maybe.' We mold our capabilities to meet the needs of our clients. We support professionals who work in demanding professions and sometimes require the near impossible. We enjoy meeting those kinds of challenges. It's satisfying to know when you've helped a client succeed." ∎

OFFICE SERVICES AND
RECEPTION AREA.

16

REAL ESTATE, DEVELOPMENT & CONSTRUCTION

PHOTO BY LARRY GEDDIS

RUSSELL DEVELOPMENT COMPANY, INC.

The work of Portland developer and property manager John W. Russell is a personal statement that at once defines the unique qualities of the Portland urban environment and explains the commercial success of Russell Development Co.

During his career, Russell has been involved with the development and management of nine commercial structures in downtown Portland involving 1.5 million feet of commercial space valued at more than $250 million.

One of Russell's first major commercial developments, Pacwest Center, has been heralded by New York's *Wall Street Journal* as one of the ten best skyscrapers in America.

THE THOMAS MANN BUILDING, BY COMBINING RETAIL, OFFICE, AND HOUSING, WAS A PIONEER IN 1980 OF MULTIPLE USES.

Russell Development Co. projects are consistently recognized for design excellence, architectural innovation, sensitive renovation of existing structures, and energy efficiency. Occupancy rates in Russell's buildings consistently outpace metropolitan area averages. And the high occupancy is achieved at premium lease rates.

Through his personal guidance with the Chamber of Commerce, the Portland Planning Commission, Portland Development Commission, and Oregon Transportation Commission, Russell has helped for more than 20 years to establish the framework for a Portland downtown renowned for its vibrancy and livability.

But if you ask him, he'll modestly explain that Russell Development Co. is simply in the "project business–doing one great building at a time."

Russell launched his company in 1979 after selling his interests in Melvin Mark Properties where he served for ten years as partner and general manager. His company's first project was the renovation of a 65,000-square-foot historic property, which featured a retail toy store on the ground floor, two floors of attorney's offices, and eight apartment units above. By today's standards the configuration of retail, office, and residential space in one commercial structure seems unremarkable, but twenty years ago the multiple-use concept was virtually unheard of on the West Coast.

PACWEST CENTER'S GLOWING ALUMINUM FACADE MAKES AN ELEGANT STATEMENT ON PORTLAND'S SKYLINE.

Although he was raised in the Pacific Northwest, Russell's design reflected his fascination with New York City's SoHo District and foresaw the popularity of loft living that downtown Portlanders now take for granted.

The project received a HUD Action Grant and one of four national HUD awards for design. For more than twenty years, since the building's opening, it has remained at full occupancy—testimony to the financial feasibility of the concept.

The project also gave Russell the opportunity to demonstrate the workability of an idea he believes in so strongly that he calls it a passion: the importance of a strong first floor retail presence. First floor retail has been a hallmark of every Russell development since.

Said Russell, "The concept of a vital and attractive ground floor matters not only to the building, but to the city as well. I think it's what makes the difference between cities and suburbs."

In 1980, Russell Development was given a consulting assignment by an Oregon bank to develop a headquarters building on a full block in downtown Portland. Russell arranged for the acquisition of fee interest of the land, selected Hugh Stubbins (the famed chair of Harvard's school of architecture) as architect, supervised the preliminary design process, and obtained an unprecedented variance on the site for additional height and density. Russell selected Hoffman Construction as his builder, a relationship that has continued in most of his projects.

Russell then partnered with Morstan Development Company, a subsidiary of Morgan Stanley, and the two companies were able to persuade Japanese companies to provide both interim and permanent financing for the project. Thus, Pacwest Center became the first major office development in the United States to utilize Japanese equity funds.

THE 200 MARKET BUILDING (LOWER LEFT) IS A GARDEN OASIS ON MARKET STREET. THE FECHHEIMER BUILDING (LOWER RIGHT) IS ONE OF THE BEST EXAMPLES IN AMERICA OF CAST-IRON FACADES.

Russell's company was then named as development manager and management/leasing agent for the project. Russell faced difficult competition for tenants from two prominent buildings, both of which were taller and both of which had started construction earlier. Nevertheless, Russell's building opened in 1984 at 80 percent occupancy–compared to 40 and 20 percent for the other two.

By every measure–local reaction, national acclaim, and lease rate/occupancy ratios–Pacwest Center was an overwhelming success. Why? Well, in the words of the *Wall Street Journal* when they named the tower as one of the ten best in the nation, because Russell "fretted over it like a new baby."

Russell said that his personal, total hands-on approach to development and the personal passion he brings to it make a difference that has value for tenants.

"Office buildings are rarely undertaken by professionals–they're usually done by corporations. We do everything–financing, design, construction, leasing. Since I was responsible for everything, I could relate every detail to potential tenants," he explained.

His own particular brand of genius that emerged during this project was Russell's ability to understand the marketing aspect of building. He said he took the beauty that architect Stubbins contributed to the project and translated that beauty into value. Said Russell, "Stubbins was a genius at design, but that is not the sum total of successful commercial development."

Russell's ability to find value was tested again when he was approached in 1988 to purchase the 200 Market Building. Affectionately known to Portlanders as the "Black Box," the building had been for sale for a long period of time because it contained asbestos in its fireproofing; frankly, everyone was afraid to touch it. Russell's company arranged for and managed the asbestos abatement program–the first time such a task had been undertaken in a large, multi-tenanted office building. He upgraded the lobby and first floor with his

signature retail emphasis. He allowed tenants to redesign their own spaces. In 1990, Blue Cross and Blue Shield of Oregon became a major tenant in the building and half-owner. Russell has remained as a general partner and the managing agent.

Now as Russell's interest focuses on property management, his philosophy of finding market value continues to serve tenants well. "Not every tenant can deal directly with an owner," Russell pointed out. "They are looking for custom tailored solutions to sophisticated needs, and absentee owners can't always fill the bill.

"Our buildings get better every year. Some people accept the premise that buildings lose value and relevancy over time–that doesn't have to be the case. It takes investment, though, and tenants can feel that. We invest continuously in our buildings."

As to the future, Russell says he looks forward to the next challenging project. And, in the meantime, he is pleased with the direction he sees his city taking.

"Portland's civic leaders have recognized that development is a complex puzzle and all the parts need to be in place. Our geography–a downtown core that is hemmed in by the Willamette River on one side and the West Hills on the other– prevented the sprawl that other cities have endured, but I believe that we in Portland also have an ethic that is simply different and better. The ethic is a pride of place, and our downtown reflects that pride." ■

PACWEST CENTER WAS
NAMED BY *THE WALL
STREET JOURNAL*
AS ONE OF THE TEN
BEST OFFICE TOWERS
IN AMERICA.

GROUP MACKENZIE

G roup Mackenzie is a multi-disciplined architectural and engineering design firm that has literally come of age with the Portland metropolitan community. Since 1960 when it was first established, the firm has successfully grown and evolved from a simple two-person structural engineering office to a company of more than 100 full-time professionals. The group has developed a reputation throughout the West Coast for innovative approaches to complex commercial and industrial development. The group's goal is to create value for client, community, and company by providing the highest quality design services.

TOP: PG&E CORPORATE OFFICE, PORTLAND. RIGHT: LOBBY OF ORCAD, TIGARD.

Group Mackenzie offers clients highly personalized service through the utilization of dedicated teams backed by the resources of the larger firm. Each team provides interdisciplinary expertise in its specific focus, including corporate campus design, high tech and industrial manufacturing, project development, corporate relocation, site selection, and tenant programming.

The team approach gives Group Mackenzie flexibility and the ability to move quickly to meet client needs. Teams provide cost-effective value to customers for projects of any size.

When Tom Mackenzie began providing engineering services more than forty years ago, few people could have foreseen the changes that would occur in Oregon. Since 1960, Portland's population has grown almost 30 percent, from 372,000 to more than half a million. The suburban area has literally exploded: Tualatin has grown from 365 people in 1960 to its current population of more than 21,000; Hillsboro from 4,000 to 70,000; Beaverton from 6,000 to 68,000.

The community is much more "internationalized." In the past decade, high tech products have surpassed timber and agricultural goods as the region's leading exports. The number of companies in the area has doubled since 1960 to more than 50,000.

All of this has changed the rules of development. Now, as Group Mackenzie executives point out, the region has shifted to a more urban-focused development philosophy. Rather than "green field" development, clients are usually dealing with redevelopment and infill. Infrastructure issues more severely impact cost and project feasibility. Oregonians, by choice and regulatory necessity, have become more sensitive to environmental issues. Communities have become more involved stakeholders.

To help clients deal successfully in this new environment, Group Mackenzie combines its long-term relationships and knowledge of the community with a constant vigilance for the new disciplines and approaches required to respond to changes. In response to client needs, the group's comprehensive list of in-house services has grown to include more than 18 specialties including everything from interior design to seismic upgrading to sustainable design to traffic analysis to value engineering to regional planning and public involvement strategies.

The firm maintains strong relationships with all municipalities and is intimately knowledgeable of zoning and land use issues. Through its involvement on local planning and advisory committees, Group Mackenzie is helping to set high standards for the future. The firm's professionals are actively involved on the Washington Square Regional Planning Commission, the North Macadam "brownfield" project,

the City of Portland Urban Renewal Advisory Committee, and the Central City Transportation Committee, to name a few.

Despite the changing landscape, there is one fundamental skill that continues to be the basis for Group Mackenzie's success: "We listen better. We don't believe a project is a success unless it's actually built. We want clients to be nothing less than thrilled when they move in," explains Mackenzie president Jeff Reaves.

The group's client list attests to its ability to deliver. Group Mackenzie's hundreds of clients are helping to reshape the face of the greater Portland community. Just a few examples: Group Mackenzie has developed corporate campuses in cooperation with Novellus Systems, In Focus, and PG&E. High tech clients include Tokyo Electron, Mitsubishi Silicon, and RadiSys. Group Mackenzie has assisted in the corporate relocation of companies like public relations giant Waggener-Edstrom, Corillian, and OrCad. They've helped with efforts to diversify Oregon's economy through the design and engineering work of industrial manufacturing projects for Welded Tube, JV Northwest, and Warn Industries.

Group Mackenzie's accomplishments also include notable projects which demonstrate the philosophy of creating "community icons" to set the tone for neighborhoods where they are located. It is no coincidence that Mackenzie projects like the East Portland Community Policing Center have become the heart of renewed neighborhoods. In that case, what started as a police station evolved into a mixed-use center for the neighborhood through a creative partnership that included the city, an interested developer, and local businesses.

Group Mackenzie believes that the best is yet to come for Oregon's already dynamic economic environment. The firm is well on the way toward helping the business community prepare to meet the challenges of future growth. Look to Group Mackenzie in coming years for creative solutions to constrained site design, sustainable building, transportation systems that work, and structures that maintain the identity of the communities they've helped to build for more than 40 years. ■ *To learn more about Group Mackenzie, please visit www.groupmackenzie.com.*

TOP: EAST PORTLAND COMMUNITY POLICING CENTER, PORTLAND. LEFT: THE DEDICATED STAFF OF PROFESSIONALS AT GROUP MACKENZIE.

NORRIS, BEGGS & SIMPSON

From the day it opened for business in 1932, Norris, Beggs & Simpson has played a key role in Pacific Northwest commercial real estate. While the company's original focus was property management and brokerage, it quickly expanded into commercial mortgage lending. A premier commercial real estate agency in its region, Norris, Beggs & Simpson ranked number one on The Portland Business Journal's 2001 list of top 25 commercial real estate firms, top 25 commercial property management firms, and most active commercial mortgage companies in the area.

With over 120 employees, and offices in Portland, Oregon and Vancouver and Bellevue, Washington, the company serves clients' needs in Oregon, Washington, Idaho, Northern California, and Nevada. Each office is managed and staffed by key decision makers, individuals whose years of knowledge and experience in a particular discipline of commercial real estate are marked by expertise and commitment.

While firmly established in the Pacific Northwest, Norris, Beggs & Simpson can also assist clients with their global real estate needs. As a member of New America International, the world's largest affiliation of major independent commercial, industrial, and investment real estate brokerage firms, Norris, Beggs & Simpson has access to more than 3,000 commercial real estate professionals in over 230 offices worldwide, covering 48 states, and 22 countries.

THE FIRST NORRIS, BEGGS & SIMPSON OFFICE. THE WILCOX BUILDING, SOUTHWEST SIXTH AND WASHINGTON, PORTLAND, OREGON—1932.

Norris, Beggs & Simpson has represented buyers and sellers, landlords and tenants, and developers and investors in the area's top regional landmarks. ODS Tower and Liberty Center, the KOIN Tower, 100 Columbia, Cornell Oaks, and Bank of America Financial Center are among the major commercial projects. The relationship formed with their clients is one of integrity and credibility. Much of the company's success can be attributed to their mission which is to learn their clients' industry and business and maintain a deep understanding of their goals.

Long ago, the company realized the best way to help its clients succeed was to offer a vertically integrated selection of services. The company's progressive approach has enabled it to survive the unpredictability of the real estate business, and ultimately to thrive in the 21st century. The firm has developed a breadth of experience in the following disciplines:

• Brokerage: Associates at Norris, Beggs & Simpson specialize in office, industrial, and retail sales and leasing, as well as investment, multifamily, and land sales. Its Capital Asset Group focuses on the sale of institutional-grade investment and plant-site opportunities.

• Mortgage Banking: The real estate finance department has a highly qualified loan origination staff, geared to satisfy the lending or borrowing needs and investment production requirements of their clients. Through an extensive correspondent network, Norris, Beggs & Simpson has access to billions of dollars from major life insurance companies, pension funds, conduits, and real estate investment trusts. The Loan Administration Department, comprised of servicing, closing, and ongoing administrative services, aids our finance officers. The veteran loan administration personnel are supported by sophisticated accounting/servicing programs that allow the quick and efficient response necessary to ensure their lenders' asset(s) are secure and viable.

• Asset/Property Management: Norris, Beggs & Simpson is an accredited management organization (AMO). Its professional staff has received certification from the industry's leading real estate organizations. These professionals take a personal interest in each property whether it is office, retail, industrial, or multifamily. The Property Management Accounting Department adds extensive support by attending to all financial requirements.

• Support Services: Carrying out their goal of providing well-rounded services to their clients, Norris, Beggs & Simpson's production staff is supported by a variety of services including advertising and communications, engineering services, human resources, legal, and market research.

The ownership of Norris, Beggs & Simpson consists of five partners who are committed to active client involvement. President, J. Clayton Hering, and Executive Vice Presidents',

THE FOUNDING PARTNERS
OF NORRIS, BEGGS &
SIMPSON—1932.
FAR LEFT: A.D. NORRIS.
LEFT: GEORGE J. BEGGS.
BOTTOM: DAVID B.
SIMPSON.

Joseph F. Wood, H. Roger Qualman, and Jan Robertson are all third-generation owners, and the company's newest partner and Executive Vice President, Chris Johnson, is a fourth-generation owner.

The company prides itself on its strong community ties and company principals, as well as a staff who has a long history of active social, civic, and political involvement. Currently, the company works with such organizations as Young Audiences, Northwest Business for Culture and the Arts, Portland Symphony, Portland Oregon Visitors Association, Association for Portland Progress, and Portland Development Commission, to name a few.

Norris, Beggs & Simpson sees itself as an extension of each client: an entire staff of experienced professionals working in partnership for the best interests of their clients as they monitor ever-shifting markets and emerging trends.

With a motto of "local focus, international reach," Norris, Beggs & Simpson is dedicated to providing the market knowledge and resources their clients require to be successful in today's market. The business is evolving in all directions as young, vital professionals are brought on board. Norris, Beggs & Simpson is optimistic about being well positioned in growth markets due to the quality of life in the Pacific Northwest. Wise in terms of history, the company constantly looks toward the future in this rapidly changing real estate industry. ∎

AMBERGLEN BUSINESS CENTER / BIRTCHER COMMERCIAL DEVELOPMENT GROUP

AMBERGLEN OFFERS A FULL SPECTRUM OF BUSINESS FACILITIES FROM CORPORATE OFFICES TO RESEARCH AND DEVELOPMENT OR LIGHT MANUFACTURING.

How did AmberGlen Business Center become the hub of the region's fastest growing, high tech-focused Sunset Corridor? Birtcher Properties, developer and manager of the area's leading West Side development, believes that you begin by throwing out all the long held perceptions of impersonal, suburban sprawl and replace them with some forward thinking that focuses on people and their desired lifestyle. Then combine some of the best elements of urban development in a new configuration, unconstrained by outdated infrastructure. The end product is uniquely Northwest.

Consequently, Portland, long known for its vital downtown core, is emerging with a well-deserved reputation for its unusually thoughtful suburban communities. AmberGlen and Birtcher Properties are in the forefront of that evolution.

Jim Edwards, Senior Vice President for Birtcher at AmberGlen Business Center, believes that AmberGlen reflects a more mature, long-term approach to development.

AMBERGLEN'S PICTURESQUE 217-ACRE CAMPUS SETTING AFFORDS BUSINESS TENANTS AND THEIR EMPLOYEES AN ACTIVE, PRODUCTIVE ENVIRONMENT.

"AmberGlen embodies so much of what we've learned about building a planned environment that will evolve and age well, rather than a creation of dated obsolescence and continuous 'recycling'." AmberGlen currently offers 1.3 million square feet of mixed office space and flex-buildings with plans for an additional 900,000 square feet. As the largest office park in Oregon, AmberGlen at 217-acres, also gives Birtcher the unique opportunity to protect its ambience.

"The most important aspect of real estate development is people," Edwards says, "and especially in an area where the challenge is to attract world-class minds, the workplace can become one of the enticements or recruiting tools. With our proximity to institutions like the Oregon Health and Sciences University's west campus we can actually serve as an enhancement to the development of Oregon's biotechnology and biomedical industry."

One has only to view the sweeping green lawns, two and three story classic brick structures, and water features of AmberGlen's spacious central commons to get a sense of what Edwards is talking about.

Throughout the West Coast, Birtcher Properties has demonstrated a formula for success. But don't confuse that thought process with cloning, cautions Edwards. As he explains, Birtcher understands the importance of differentiating to meet the criteria to be one of the office complex "nodes" within a metropolitan area. The basis for a development's appeal is to identify the appropriate employment concentration for a location and the support structures it requires: services, housing, retail, transportation, and amenities appropriate to the makeup of the specific workforce. Recognizing and enhancing that mix, says Edwards, is one of the keys to AmberGlen's continued success and the success of thoughtful long-term development in the Portland metropolitan area. ■

WRG DESIGN, INC.

WRG Design, Inc. is one of an elite circle of design firms that has helped to create Oregon's reputation for progressive and thoughtful use of its land and natural resources. During a decade of unparalleled growth in the state, the firm's commitment to the livability of the communities has set the tone for some of the region's most notable development projects.

WRG Design is a multi-disciplined firm that takes a holistic approach to land use planning, surveying, master planning, civil engineering, landscape architecture, and project management.

Founded in 1991, primarily as a civil engineering firm, the group has grown to include more than 100 employees, with offices located in Portland, Oregon (where the firm is headquartered), Las Vegas, Nevada, and Phoenix, Arizona.

WRG established a reputation for excellence with its first project when the group provided environmental and engineering guidance to the developers of Skamania Lodge—a 100-acre destination resort located in the scenic Columbia River Gorge. They proved themselves again assisting AmberJack and Birtcher Development with AmberGlen Business Center, one of the Northwest's largest business parks located at the heart of Oregon's high-tech centered Sunset Corridor. And during the ensuing decade WRG has amassed a respected list of clients both public and private including the area's major commercial

developers, Home Depot, Fred Meyer, Gramor, and residential developers like Centex Homes, Matrix, and Ryland Homes. At any one time the firm may have as many as 350 projects in progress.

Because sports facilities such as the award winning Hillsboro Sports Complex are also a special niche for the group, it is no surprise that the owners approach business with the passion, competitive spirit, and sense of fun of a winning athletic team.

What is WRG's formula for success? Managing Partner Darren Welborn says that he and Jon Reimann—the original partners—founded the company at a time when technology was creating massive changes in their industry. "We were able to build our organization from the start to fit the times: aggressive, quicker pace, more flexibility to meet change, a higher level of professionalism," Welborn explained.

"When we hire we look for people who take their work personally—who treat their client's money like it was their own. People who have a passion for approaching projects in a manner that not only benefits the client but also makes our community a better place to live," Welborn explained. "We work hard, there's no doubt about that, but we were lucky to start our company in a growing and prosperous city like Portland." ■

LEFT: BEN WILLIAMS, PE, PRINCIPAL, WORKS CLOSELY WITH CLIENTS ON THE FRONT END OF A PROJECT TO ASSESS THE FEASIBILITY OF A SITE AND ITS POTENTIAL FOR DEVELOPMENT.

BOTTOM: MLK BOULEVARD/GRAND AVENUE STREETSCAPE DESIGN WAS ONE OF PORTLAND'S "TOP PROJECTS." IT HAS LED TO A GROUND SWELL OF URBAN REDEVELOPMENT IN THIS HISTORIC EASTSIDE DISTRICT.

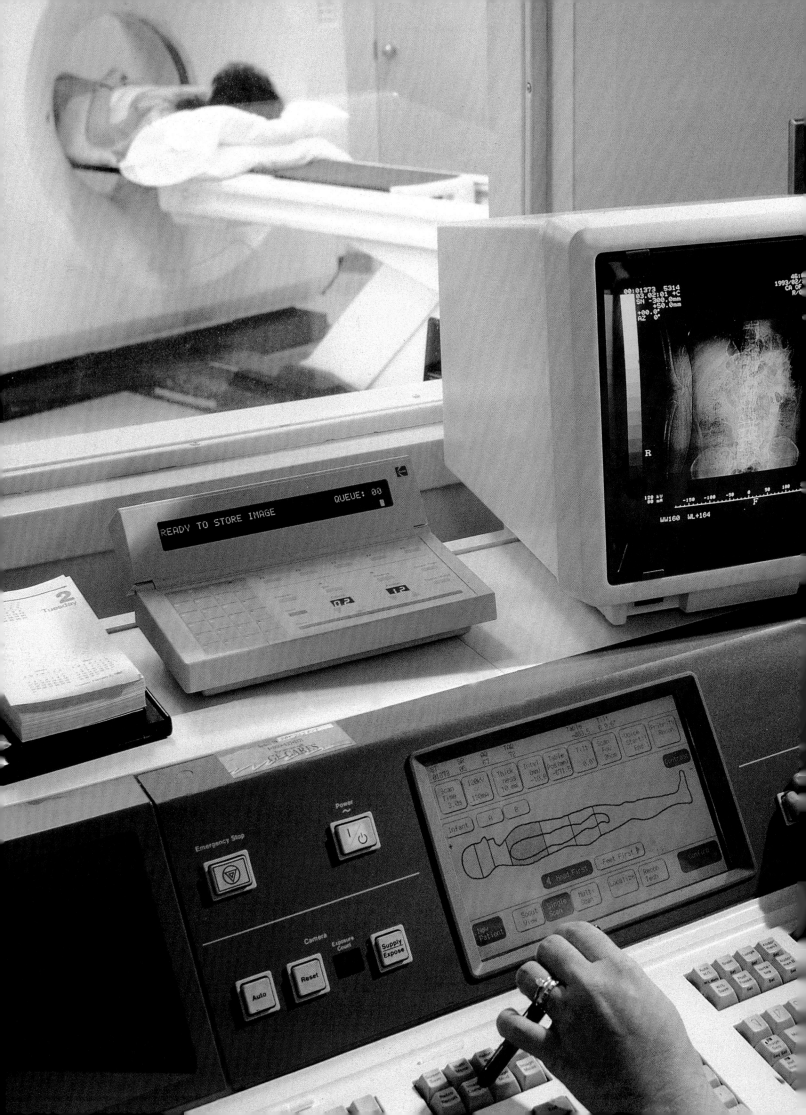

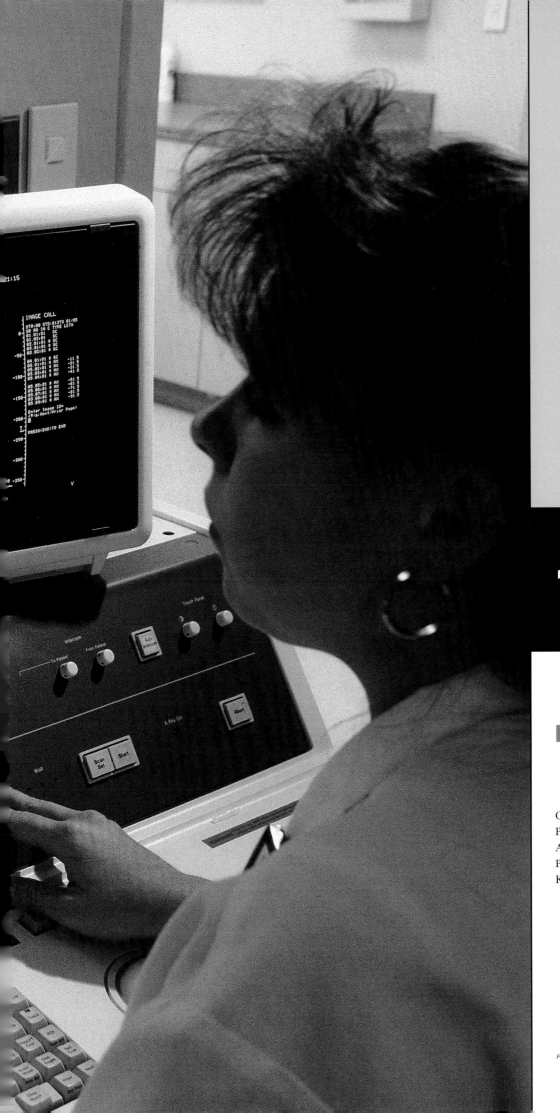

17

HEALTH CARE

PHOTO BY ROBERT FOUTS

OREGON HEALTH & SCIENCE UNIVERSITY

DOERNBECHER CHILDREN'S HOSPITAL OFFERS THE WIDEST RANGE OF CHILDREN'S HEALTH CARE SERVICES IN THE REGION. FROM PRIMARY CARE TO THE MOST SOPHISTICATED TREATMENTS DEVELOPED AS A RESULT OF EXTENSIVE RESEARCH, DOERNBECHER IS A HAVEN FOR OREGON'S YOUNGEST CITIZENS—AS WELL AS FOR MANY CHILDREN FROM OUTSIDE OREGON. *PHOTO BY DONALD HAMILTON*

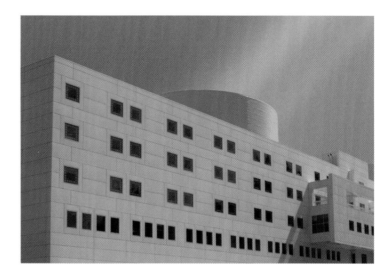

Oregon Health & Science University (OHSU) is the region's preeminent health science teaching, research, and patient care center. Nationally recognized for its standards of quality, OHSU includes top ranked Schools of Dentistry, Medicine, and Nursing; OHSU Hospital; Doernbecher Children's Hospital; numerous primary-care and specialty clinics; multiple research institutes and centers; and more than 200 outreach and public service programs that serve the entire state of Oregon.

For more than 100 years, Oregonians have enjoyed the highest quality, most advanced care possible thanks to OHSU's presence in the community. OHSU provides the full spectrum of health care, from routine services to complex and revolutionary specialty treatments available no place else on the West Coast.

OHSU's patients—treated at its 116-acre Marquam Hill campus and satellite clinics throughout the state—are as diverse as Oregon's population. Each year, more than 153,000 patients who make more than 600,000 visits annually are treated at OHSU—a third of them children. OHSU makes a substantial commitment and financial contribution to the care of Oregon's sickest, most vulnerable and underserved citizens, including individuals with cultural and language

barriers, inner-city, and rural residents. More low-income patients are treated by OHSU than any other health system or hospital in the state.

More than four-fifths of OHSU's 400 hospital beds are filled at any given time, and almost a quarter of the babies born at the hospital are the result of high-risk pregnancies that require the newborns to be hospitalized after delivery.

As the state's fourth largest corporate employer, and Portland's largest, OHSU fuels more economic activity and generates more jobs than most other corporations and organizations in the state. More than 36,000 jobs throughout Oregon are created by the university's activities with more than a $2 billion economic impact.

Additionally, OHSU attracts nearly a quarter of a billion dollars in out-of-state money to Oregon each year—nearly four times what OHSU receives in state appropriation support. Much of this revenue takes the form of research grants, which have quadrupled in the past ten years.

OHSU's recent efforts to bring together traditional biosciences with cutting-edge technology for research and patient treatment holds the potential for placing Oregon on the international leading edge of biomedical and biotechnical research in the next generation. A recent merger between OHSU and the highly respected Oregon Graduate Institute of Science and Technology created the new OGI School of Science and Engineering at OHSU. Through this action, OHSU hopes to become the driving force behind the creation of a stable biotech cluster in the state.

OHSU'S MARQUAM HILL CAMPUS TODAY SHOWS THE REMARKABLE GROWTH THE INSTITUTION HAS ACHIEVED. MUCH OF THAT GROWTH HAS BEEN IN THE LAST 15 YEARS. IN TOTAL, OHSU OCCUPIES 5 MILLION SQUARE FEET OF SPACE VALUED AT MORE THAN A BILLION DOLLARS. HOSPITALS AND CLINICS OCCUPY 27 PERCENT OF THE SPACE; RESEARCH, 22 PERCENT; EDUCATION, 21 PERCENT; INSTITUTIONAL SUPPORT AND ADMINISTRATION, EIGHT PERCENT; AND PARKING STRUCTURES, 22 PERCENT. *PHOTO BY DONALD HAMILTON*

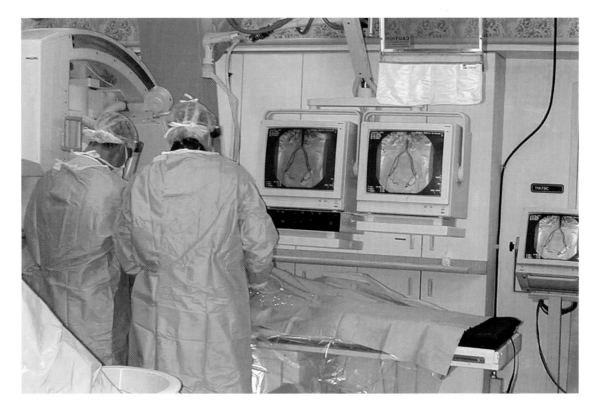

TOP: THE DOTTER INSTITUTE, THE FIRST CENTER DEDICATED SOLELY TO INTERVENTIONAL RADIOLOGY, UTILIZES VIDEOCONFERENCING TECHNOLOGY TO BRING SCIENTISTS WORLDWIDE UP TO DATE ON THE LATEST DEVELOPMENTS IN THE FIELD. *PHOTO BY SHERI IMAI-SWIGGART*

Throughout its history, OHSU has been gifted with visionary leadership that has positioned the institution to meet the needs of Oregonians through a dynamic synergism of activities that focus in four areas: patient care, research, education, and community outreach.

Oregon Health & Science University traces its roots back to 1867, as Salem, Oregon's Willamette University Medical Department. In 1913, the Department merged with University of Oregon's Portland-based medical school to become the only medical school in the Pacific Northwest.

More than half a century later, in 1974, the creation of the University of Oregon Health Sciences Center brought the University of Oregon's schools of dentistry, medicine, and nursing together as a single institution. The unification made OHSU the state's only academic health center, one of 125 medical centers in the country, and one of only 20 not affiliated with a larger university.

In 1995, OHSU became a public corporation, independent for the first time from the Oregon State System of Higher Education. Instead, the institution is governed by the OHSU Board of Directors, whose members are appointed by the governor and confirmed by the State Senate. OHSU's new structure has allowed the university to respond with greater speed to changing market conditions, enabling it to more effectively accomplish its mission.

According to the National Research Corporation, local health-care consumers rank OHSU as the metropolitan-area hospital with the best physicians and reputation. In a study, which rated 2,500 hospitals nationwide, OHSU ranked number one in Oregon for highest quality of health-care services, staff, and image.

BOTTOM: OHSU AND THE OREGON GRADUATE INSTITUTE OF SCIENCE AND TECHNOLOGY JOINED FORCES IN JULY 2000. BOTH INSTITUTIONS WILL BENEFIT FROM THE MERGER AT A TIME WHEN THE NEED FOR COLLABORATION BETWEEN HEALTH SCIENCES AND TECHNOLOGY BECOMES MORE AND MORE APPARENT. THESE BENEFITS RANGE FROM THE DESIGN OF NEW MEDICAL INSTRUMENTATION TO THE DEVELOPMENT OF BIOINFORMATICS DATABASES TO THE CREATION OF NEW SOFTWARE FOR RESEARCH AND PATIENT CARE. THE MERGER ALSO IS EXPECTED TO ASSIST OGI IN EXPANDING ITS COMPUTER SCIENCE, ELECTRICAL ENGINEERING, COMPUTER ENGINEERING, AND ENVIRONMENTAL SCIENCE PROGRAMS. *PHOTO BY DAVID MOORE*

Several specific programs have contributed to OHSU's reputation. The Oregon Cancer Institute at OHSU is one of 60 centers designated by the National Cancer Institute of the National Institutes of Health, and the only one in Oregon. Each year 2,800 new patients, many of whom are newly diagnosed with cancer, turn to OHSU for their cancer care. OHSU's unique combination of research, education, and direct care provides patients with unique access to some of the newest advances in cancer treatment, diagnosis, and prevention.

The University also is carving out a reputation for itself as a regional resource for cardiac care. Averaging more than 1,100 procedures per year, OHSU's physicians and researchers are nationally recognized experts who offer care in every aspect of cardiology, cardiothoracic surgery, pediatric cardiothoracic surgery, and cardiac catheterization.

The widest range of children's health-care services in the Pacific Northwest is to be found at OHSU's Doernbecher Children's Hospital. Seventy percent of all pediatric cancer care in Oregon takes place there, and it is the primary source for unique clinical services such as organ transplants, treatment of serious injuries, and neonatal intensive care.

OHSU's trauma center, one of two in the metropolitan area, was recently recognized by the *Journal of the American Medical Association* as one of the top trauma center models in the United States.

Looking to the needs of an aging population, the university has established the interdepartmental Center for Healthy Aging.

OHSU holds that the avenue to providing excellent care is by training the best health-care professionals to be found. In addition to receiving the highest marks granted by the nation's major accrediting organizations, the university's three professional schools have been recognized as among the top in the nation by its peers:

• OHSU's School of Medicine is ranked in the top two percent of American medical schools for its primary-care education program, an honor bestowed on it for the past five years by *U.S. News & World Report.* Of 144 schools reported, OHSU also ranked fourth for excellence in family medicine and eighth for the specialty of rural medicine.

• OHSU's Dental Program, which turns out almost 90 percent of Oregon's dentists, consistently attracts applicants whose grade-point average rank it among the top 10 dental schools in the United States.

• The OHSU School of Nursing graduate programs are ranked in the

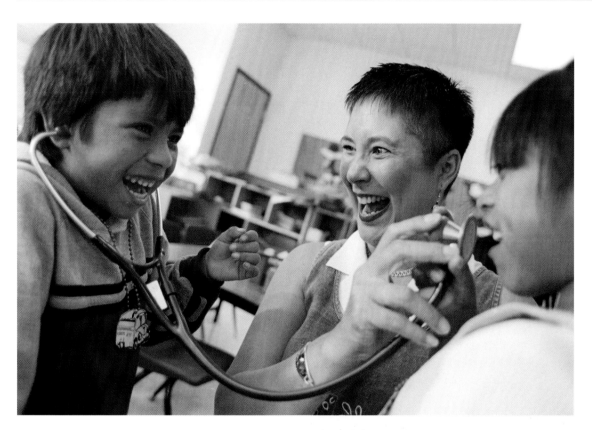

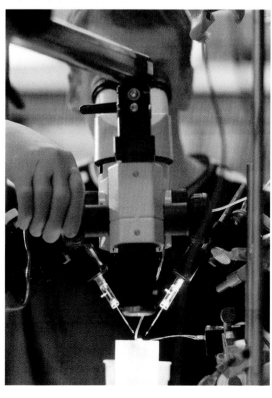

top two percent for excellence and quality among more than 350 such programs in the nation as reported by *U.S. News & World Report.* All seven of its graduate specialty areas scored in the top ten.

OHSU recognizes that in today's fast changing world of health care, continuing education is a necessity. Last year, more than 20,000 health-care professionals took part in continuing education opportunities provided by OHSU. By satellite transmission, off-site classes, and the Internet, OHSU serves these professionals by reaching them where they are.

In recent years, OHSU researchers have announced a clinical breakthrough at a rate of one every seven days. This may explain why OHSU ranks 34th among the more than 2,400 institutions competing for research dollars. OHSU's sponsored research has grown by more than 1,000 percent since 1984, from $14 million to $168 million. OHSU has recently announced plans for a biomedical research campaign to raise $500 million in public and private funds over the next seven years. The goal is to make OHSU one of the top medical research centers in the United States.

Spearheaded by this effort, Oregon Health & Science University will continue to lead the way to ensure that all Oregonians will have access to the highest quality of health care and education today and in the future. ■

TOP: OHSU HAS TEAMED UP WITH COMMUNITIES, FOUNDATIONS, AND FEDERAL AND STATE LAWMAKERS TO STRENGTHEN THE EDUCATION AND HEALTH CARE SYSTEMS IN OREGON. OHSU OFFERS SEVERAL PROGRAMS TO MEET THE INCREASING NEED FOR PRIMARY CARE PRACTITIONERS, INCLUDING PHYSICIANS, PHYSICIAN ASSISTANTS, AND NURSE PRACTITIONERS. OTHER OHSU PROGRAMS HELP CORRECT IMBALANCES IN OREGONIANS' GEOGRAPHIC OR FINANCIAL ACCESS TO HEALTH CARE. *PHOTO BY RICK RAPPAPORT*

BOTTOM: UNIVERSITY SCIENTISTS HAVE INTRODUCED MORE THAN 400 INVENTIONS SINCE 1985, AND MORE THAN 15 COMPANIES HAVE BEEN SPUN OFF BASED ON OHSU-DISCOVERED TECHNOLOGIES. IN THE DEPARTMENT OF PHYSIOLOGY AND PHARMACOLOGY IN OHSU'S SCHOOL OF MEDICINE, A RESEARCHER BRINGS THE PRINCIPLES OF ELECTRICAL ENGINEERING AND MOLECULAR BIOLOGY TO BEAR ON THE STUDY OF THE PROTEIN THAT IS DEFECTIVE IN THE GENETIC DISEASE CYSTIC FIBROSIS. *PHOTO BY RICK RAPPAPORT*

PORTLAND VETERANS AFFAIRS MEDICAL CENTER

Portland is a community that proudly honors its veterans. From the beautiful and serene Vietnam Veterans Memorial at Washington Park to the National Cemetery in Southeast Portland, the community recognizes the courage and sacrifice of those who have helped to keep our country free.

TOP: THE CAMPUS OF THE PORTLAND VA MEDICAL CENTER, LOCATED ON MARQUAM HILL, OVERLOOKING THE CITY OF PORTLAND. RIGHT: RONALD BARRY, PH.D., IS AN IMMUNOLOGIST WHO STUDIES WAYS TO DEVELOP VACCINES TO FIGHT INFECTIOUS DISEASES. HE ALSO STUDIES THE HEPATITIS C VIRUS (PICTURED WITH TINA CLARK, RESEARCH ASSISTANT). PHOTO BY MICHAEL MOODY

But while many monuments serve as a reminder for future generations, the Portland Veterans Affairs (VA) Medical Center honors veterans in a very immediate and fundamental way: working today to improve their health and well-being. And it's a big job when you consider that almost half of all Americans who ever served during wartime in our country's history are alive today.

The Portland VA Medical Center serves as the major referral point for the U. S. Department of Veterans Affairs health administration activities in Oregon, Southern Washington and parts of Idaho. It is organized into two divisions. The Portland Division includes the medical center located atop Marquam Hill on 28 acres over-looking the city, and the Vancouver Division is located 11 miles north in Vancouver, Washington. Until 1980, Vancouver was the site for Vancouver VA Hospital, which was consolidated into the Portland medical center. The two facilities have a total of 288 beds.

Vancouver is also headquarters for the Veterans Integrated Service Network (VISN) 20, an organizational structure that integrates service delivery in a larger region stretching from Alaska, throughout the entire state of Washington including the Puget Sound, and into Oregon as far south as Medford. The objective of the VISN is to better coordinate the continuum of health care.

The Portland VA Medical Center is a tertiary care facility, providing a full range of integrated services including primary and long-term care. The medical center is the region's referral center for acute medical, surgical, psychiatric, neurological, and extended care services. Specialty referral services also include blood-brain-barrier disruption; cardiology/cardiac surgery; endoscopic ultrasound; HIV treatment; the program for the homeless; seizure monitoring; sleep disorders; and women's veteran programs. Its liver transplant program serves as a resource for VA medical centers throughout the Western United States, and a new renal transplant program was recently approved.

Education is a vital component of the VA's health care mission. Portland's major academic affiliate, Oregon Health & Science University, is connected to the VA by a 660-foot sky bridge—a physical structure that effectively symbolizes the interconnectedness of the two institutions.

Each year, more than 1,200 administrative and clinical trainees receive a portion of their clinical instruction at the VA medical center. Training programs include disciplines ranging from nursing to dietetics, to alcohol and drug treatment, to dental assisting. This commitment to education in Portland is reflective of the VA's philosophical approach to the delivery of care throughout the country. Nationwide, VA medical centers are affiliated with more than 152 medical and dental schools and the VA estimates that more than half of U.S. practicing physicians have received training in VA hospitals.

In recent years the VA has made a concerted effort to reach out to the people it serves through geographically disbursed outpatient clinics and Vet Centers. The Portland VA supports community-based outpatient clinics in Bend and Salem, at the Oregon coast (Camp Rilea) and in Southern Washington (Longview). In an effort to further expand health care access for veterans, the VA soon will add two additional clinics in the Portland metropolitan area.

The Portland VA supports two Vet Centers, one in Northeast Portland and the other in Salem, located 60 miles south of the Portland Division. Readjustment counseling is offered at these sites. Vet Centers were originally designed to help Vietnam Era veterans, but with the advent of the Persian Gulf War, eligibility for counseling was expanded to include veterans who served during periods of armed hostilities following the Vietnam War. Currently, there are 205 Vet Centers nationwide. Counseling is provided for a variety of problems, including employment, marital difficulties, sexual trauma, and post-traumatic stress disorder.

Since the largest group of veterans–those who fought in World War II–is now advancing in years, it should come as no surprise that VA medical centers are known for their benchmark performance in prevention and treatment of the chronic diseases that often accompany aging. The VA is internationally recognized for the development of innovative prosthetic devices to restore function after amputations, as well as for the treatment of spinal-cord injury, mental illness, and alcoholism. The VA also is pioneering advances in patient safety, such as on-line bar-code medication administration and sophisticated computerized patient record systems that help reduce the chance of medical errors.

ED NEUWELT, MD, RESEARCHED WAYS TO DELIVER CHEMOTHERAPEUTIC DRUGS TO TUMORS IN THE BRAIN. *PHOTO BY MICHAEL MOODY*

In addition to compassionate patient care and education for tomorrow's health care providers, research is an important part of the VA mission. The Portland VA is home to an exciting research program that began in the early 1970s with a small group of scientists and clinicians dedicated to improving the health of veterans. In 1987, the newly constructed hospital provided laboratory space and state of the art equipment that ushered in a period of research growth that continues today. Portland now ranks among the top 10 VA medical centers nationwide in VA research support.

The program has more than 120 funded investigators and a budget for fiscal year 2000 that totaled nearly $22 million. Established under federal legislation allowing VAs to develop non-profit corporations, The Portland VA Research Foundation has become an invaluable asset and in 2000 handled over $7 million in funds to support research.

The strong affiliation with Oregon Health & Science University was greatly enhanced in 1993 with the opening of the sky bridge, and research collaborations continue to grow. Reflecting the critical mass of talent assembled at the medical center, the VA and the Foundation have been fortunate to receive a number of large grants in recent years to establish special centers focusing on important diseases. These include:

• Portland Environmental Hazards Research Center (1994). As one of three VA-funded centers to study unexplained illnesses of Gulf War veterans, this program focuses on potential causes of symptoms such as memory loss, fatigue, and muscle and joint pain.

• The VA Portland Alcohol Research Center (1995). Scientists at this site are among leaders in the quest to tease out the complex interplay between heredity and alcoholism, tracking down genes that may either increase or decrease risk.

CYNTHIA WAGNER, PH.D., IS AN IMMUNOLOGIST WHO STUDIES THE IMMUNE MECHANISMS OF ACUTE AND CHRONIC REJECTIONS AFTER PATIENTS HAVE RECEIVED AN ORGAN TRANSPLANT. *PHOTO BY MICHAEL MOODY*

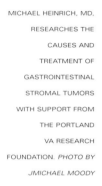

• NIH-funded Cancer Center, with affiliate OHSU (1996). In 1999, the Portland VA dedicated its newest research building, the Northwest Veterans Affairs Cancer Research Center. This facility houses joint projects of the Portland VA and OHSU, many of them on the frontiers of research to forge an entirely new generation of cancer treatments– "smart bombs" that target only cellular abnormalities underlying cancers, sparing normal tissue that can be damaged by radiation and standard chemotherapy.

• National Center for Rehabilitative Auditory Research (1997). People are often surprised to learn that the most common service-connected disability–affecting an estimated 300,000 veterans–is hearing loss. This is the only center in the VA dedicated to addressing needs of veterans with hearing loss and tinnitus, the mysterious ringing in the ears suffered by millions of Americans.

• Mental Illness Research Education and Clinical Center (1997). A collaboration with the VA Puget Sound Health Care System, this center focuses on understanding basic mechanisms, developing better treatments, and improving health services for post-traumatic stress disorder and schizophrenia–two devastating problems common among our nation's veterans.

• Research Enhancement Awards Program in Multiple Sclerosis (1999). This group is seeking new weapons against multiple sclerosis, a disabling disorder suffered by some 350,000 Americans. A recent study found that a combination treatment of estrogen and a vaccine developed by the Portland team could prevent a similar disease in female mice–a finding the researchers hope to translate to humans.

• Research Enhancement Awards Program in Hepatitis C (1999). Investigators in this program are at the forefront of

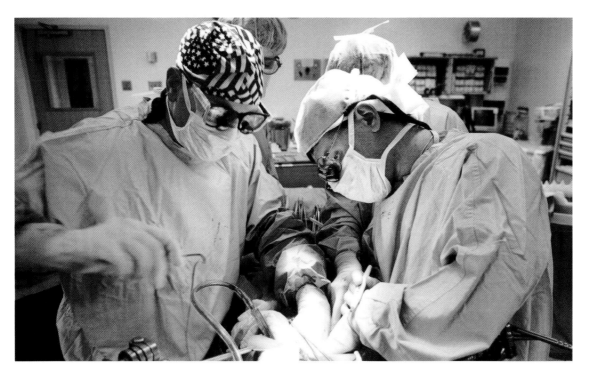

the battle against hepatitis C, a life-threatening disease that is especially common among veterans. Many recent Portland advances include progress in the work to design a vaccine, and the discovery that genetic factors in the donor liver may influence whether severe liver disease recurs in hepatitis C patients who have had a liver transplant.

• Parkinson's Disease Research Education and Clinical Center. The Portland VA gained its newest special center in 2001 when it was named one of six new VA centers specializing in Parkinson's disease, a debilitating neurological disorder that afflicts 1.5 million Americans. Research projects will include studies to determine whether deep-brain stimulation can reduce symptoms of Parkinson's disease, to find ways of regenerating brain cells damaged by the disorder, and to sort out the cause of Parkinson's-associated cognitive problems.

During the past year, investigators reported results of a number of studies with important implications for health care. For example, a Portland researcher led a large nationwide project using colonoscopy to screen the entire colon for cancer in apparently healthy people. His team found that about 10 percent of participants had colon cancer or serious precancerous growths and that at least a third of these lesions would have been missed by sigmoidoscopy—a commonly used screening technique that examines only the lower part of the colon. The results clearly showed the value of colonoscopy as a primary screening test, with enormous potential impact on colon cancer prevention and treatment.

Portland's Research Service benefits greatly from strong support of the Medical Center's Chief Executive Officer and the VISN 20 Director. With its administration's support, the quality of an expanding physical plant, and the strong association with its affiliate, Portland's research program holds the promise of many future contributions to health care for veterans and the entire community. ■

ADVENTIST MEDICAL CENTER

For more than 100 years, Adventist Medical Center has nurtured the physical, mental, and spiritual health of Portland communities by providing quality healthcare while demonstrating the healing ministry of Jesus Christ.

One of Portland's first Eastside hospitals, Adventist Medical Center was established in 1894 and to this day serves as an anchor to the Eastside community as well as Adventist's system of 14 primary care clinics located throughout Portland

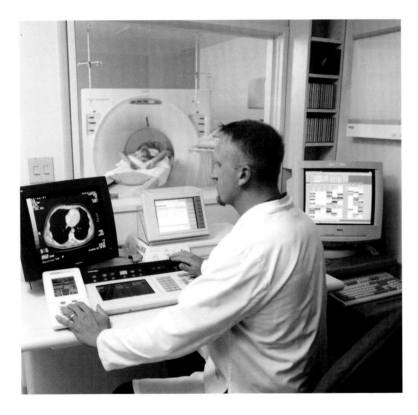

and Southwest Washington. The medical center is noted for neurosurgery, cardiology, medical imaging, and rehabilitation. With nearly 1,800 annual births, Adventist Medical Center is the birthplace of a large percentage of Eastside babies. A recent addition to the medical center campus is CherryWood Village, a 380-unit senior housing center.

Historically, Adventist healthcare has embraced a holistic approach to healthcare rooted in a long tradition of education and wellness. In the 1800s, long before it was fashionable, Seventh Day Adventist institutions were teaching the "radical" concepts of proper exercise, nutrition, and sanitation. Today, with ten of the leading causes of death lifestyle related, the message has never been more relevant and continues to be at the core of Adventist's mission. This focus on holistic care has made Adventist an active partner with over 200 area businesses in their occupational health and wellness programs.

Adventist is an active community partner as well. The Healthvan, a mobile health resource, travels throughout the community providing free and low-cost health screenings, blood pressure, cholesterol, and diabetes checks. Adventist is also involved in numerous community organizations like the Race for the Cure®, the United Way Day of Caring, and the American Heart Association.

Adventist Medical Center is part of Adventist Health, a regional system with corporate headquarters in Roseville, California. On the West Coast, Adventist Health operates over 74 outpatient sites and 20 hospitals employing more than 18,000 people. Adventist Medical Center is part of a worldwide network of hospitals founded by the Seventh-day Adventist Church. These hospitals work together to meet the challenges of a rapidly changing healthcare industry while fulfilling their mission.

This unique balance of compassion, education, clinical quality, and cost-effectiveness are the hallmarks of a system that brings one reassuring constant in an environment of relentless change—the continued ability to nurture the whole person—mind, body, and spirit. ∎

TOP: PATIENTS RECEIVE CARE FROM AN ADVANCED MEDICAL CENTER INCORPORATING RECENT TECHNOLOGICAL DEVELOPMENTS IN DIAGNOSIS AND TREATMENT OF DISEASE. RIGHT: ADVENTIST MEDICAL CENTER'S PARK-LIKE CAMPUS STRATEGICALLY LOCATED NEAR THE INTERSECTION OF INTERSTATES 205 AND 84.

PROVIDENCE HEALTH SYSTEM

More than a million people in the Portland area and throughout the State of Oregon place their trust in the health care professionals of Providence Health System–Oregon's largest health care provider and the nation's ninth leading integrated network of hospitals, health plans, clinics, and affiliated health services. The Providence family includes more than 12,500 employees, physicians, nurses and volunteers who strive to meet the health needs of Oregonians as they journey through life.

Providence owns and manages three medical centers in the metropolitan area–Providence Portland Medical Center, Providence St. Vincent Medical Center, and Providence Milwaukie Hospital. Other facilities include hospitals located in Hood River, Medford, Newberg and Seaside, Oregon; Providence Benedictine Nursing Center, a medically supervised adult living center in Mt. Angel; six specialized research centers, and dozens of medical clinics and affiliated services.

The Providence Heart Institute ranks as an international leader in cardiac care, research, and education. The institute's physicians have performed groundbreaking research in robotic-assisted surgery and advances that have led to heart valve repair and clot dissolving laser techniques.

For those whose lives have been touched by cancer, the Providence Cancer Center provides a full range of diagnostic services and treatments, pain management, counseling, and

education about prevention and early detection. Patients also are linked with additional services and support groups available in the community. A world-class team of researchers at Providence's Earle A. Chiles Research Institute and Robert W. Franz Cancer Research Center conducts innovative research.

The Providence Women and Children's Program brings focus to the multi-faceted needs of women's health care. Providence hospitals welcome more new babies than any other health care system in Oregon. Neonatal intensive care, programs for difficult pregnancies, and help for pregnant women with multiple life challenges are among the special programs available through Providence.

Long-term and end-of-life care, disease management of chronic conditions such as diabetes, and e-health, which utilizes the Internet to empower patients in the management of their own care, are among important Providence Health Plan initiatives.

"We are seeing an evolution and revolution in health care as demand for service and quality converges with rapid clinical advancements," commented Debbie Origer, Chief Strategy Officer for Providence Health System in Oregon. "Providence is investing in facilities, medical, and information technologies to insure that all Oregonians will have access to the best quality outcomes and service available."

Providence grew from the work of five Sisters of Providence who, in 1856, traveled from Montreal, Quebec, by steamship and arrived at Fort Vancouver just north of Portland. They carried westward their mission of caring for the sick and helping the poor. Despite the hardships of the frontier, the sisters persevered in their work, ultimately establishing Oregon's first hospital, St. Vincent, in 1875.

Since the pioneering sisters first set foot in the Oregon Territory, Providence has continued to be guided by five core values that remain largely unchanged: compassion, justice, respect, excellence, and stewardship. In true Christian spirit, Providence works to assure that quality care is accessible to all people, with special concern for the poor and vulnerable. ■

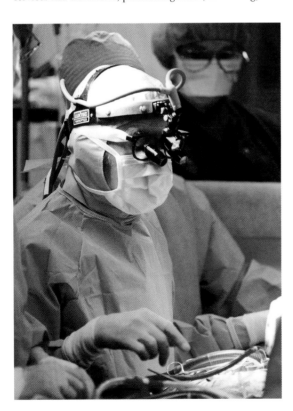

KAISER PERMANENTE

Portlander Toni Linne has entrusted her health and that of her family to Kaiser Permanente for more than 50 years.

Kaiser Permanente physicians delivered all five of Linne's children and treated them for everything from swallowing aftershave to falling out of trees.

"Help from Kaiser Permanente was always just a phone call away," she says. "We knew immediately where to find a doctor whenever someone got sick or hurt. The pediatricians our kids had were superb."

KAISER PERMANENTE MAKES AVAILABLE LOW-COST BICYCLE HELMETS FOR CHILDREN AND ADULTS AT FREQUENT SAFETY FAIRS THROUGHOUT THE COMMUNITY.

Positive experiences like Toni Linne's are the reason nearly half a million people in Oregon and Southwest Washington turn to Kaiser Permanente for quality, affordable health care.

PEOPLE HAVE BEEN CHOOSING KAISER PERMANENTE FOR THEIR HEALTH CARE NEEDS FOR MORE THAN 55 YEARS.

Kaiser Permanente, a pioneer in the delivery of prepaid health care, has deep roots in the Pacific Northwest. Kaiser Permanente's medical group was established to serve workers and their families during the construction of Grand Coulee Dam in northeastern Washington. When World War II erupted, the group provided services at the Kaiser shipyards in Portland and Vancouver, Washington. With the closing of the shipyards in 1945, enrollment was opened to the community.

Since those beginnings more than half a century ago, Kaiser Permanente has grown to become the nation's largest and most experienced health care delivery program of its kind. With care prepaid, there is no incentive to fill hospital beds; rather the incentive is to keep members healthy and satisfied.

Today, Kaiser Permanente's Northwest Region includes:
• about 700 physicians in its medical group–90 percent of whom are board certified in their specialties;
• Kaiser Sunnyside Medical Center with 196 licensed beds;
• 20 medical offices;
• over 7,400 employees; and
• one of the largest group practice dental programs in the country, with 15 dental offices serving approximately 185,000 people.

Since 1964, Kaiser Permanente's Center for Health Research has conducted groundbreaking research on disease prevention, health promotion, and cancer, and has tested new ways to organize, pay for, and deliver health care.

Kaiser Permanente has embraced technology in a way that makes health care more easily accessible to its members and increases the quality of health care delivery. Members can access medical information and services over the Internet through password-protected accounts. Physicians can call up a patient's medical history in a keystroke–and once a diagnosis is reached, they can compare the patient's personal information against the latest clinical guidelines for treating that condition.

Both individually and as an organization, the employees, physicians, and dentists of Kaiser Permanente can point to a proud history of community service. Thousands of volunteer hours, grants to non-profit groups, and surplus medical equipment donated to community organizations help improve the lives of people in the community every year.

As a new century dawns and new challenges in medicine arise, people like Kaiser Permanente member Toni Linne know the needs of their families will be met with the unique blend of compassion and professionalism Kaiser Permanente has practiced for more than half a century. ∎

PHOTO BY LARRY GEDDIS

18

THE MARKETPLACE, HOSPITALITY & TOURISM

PHOTO BY LARRY GEDDIS

AZUMANO TRAVEL

How many miles must you travel to find a company whose service standards exceed your expectations? Well, if Portland-based Azumano Travel arranges your trip, the answer might be—none. Before you set foot out the door, Azumano will have anticipated and attended to every detail of your odyssey including the needs you haven't thought of yet! With Azumano, you might well find the responsiveness you seek before the trip begins.

A business philosophy emphasizing service standards above and beyond customer expectations has led Portland-based Azumano Travel to become one of the West Coast's leading providers of global and domestic travel services.

With more than 250 employees and $150 million in annual sales, the company itself has traveled an incredible journey since the days in 1949 when founder George Azumano began booking passage on steamships for family friends who wanted to visit Japan following World War II.

Today Azumano Travel is a multi-branch, multi-faceted corporation employing seasoned travel professionals who apply the power of new technologies to help insure comfortable and hassle-free travel—at a good value—for some 250,000 business and leisure travelers each year. Azumano's nine offices extend from Vancouver in Southwest Washington through Portland, to Beaverton, Tigard, Salem, Albany, Corvallis, and Eugene.

In 2001, Azumano took the major step of becoming an American Express Travel Services Representative, effectively increasing Azumano's global presence and further extending its offerings to include the vast resources, innovative products, and financial services of a major player in the global travel industry.

A Leader In Business And Leisure Travel

Domestic business travel is at the heart of Azumano's world today. The organization—Oregon's largest travel agency—serves the business travel needs of companies ranging in size from sole proprietorships to large corporations with multi-million dollar travel budgets. Approximately 500 corporate accounts representing both private and public interests depend on Azumano for a host of travel management services.

On the leisure travel side of the equation, Azumano understands that overindulgence can be a good thing! Whether the vacation involves a Caribbean cruise, an excursion to Europe, or a weekend getaway to Las Vegas, Azumano's agents anticipate needs and lay the groundwork for thousands of dream vacations every year.

How does one company meet the needs of customers ranging from the corporate travelers of Wells Fargo Bank to newlyweds planning honeymoons?

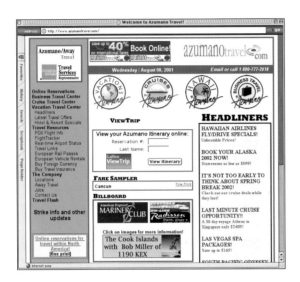

The secret to a successful working relationship, explains Azumano president and chief executive officer Sho Dozono, has everything to do with making sure there's a good fit between client and agent. Technology has greatly changed the travel industry during the past decade—in different ways for leisure and corporate travel—but Dozono believes that a high degree of personal service remains at the core of Azumano's continued success.

Consequently, Azumano focuses on hiring a good balance of travel consultants with diverse backgrounds and representing a wide cross section of the travel industry. Every travel consultant participates in intensive, ongoing training. Each is introduced to the newest systems, refreshed on standards and constantly rewarded for going the extra mile. Azumano's travel consultants average 13 years of experience—each bringing a depth of knowledge and a network of contacts that allows them to take service to the next level.

Obviously the strategy has worked.

Azumano Travel has grown dramatically through the past two decades. In 1976, it was comprised of only four travel agents. By 1987 the company was generating $24 million worth of business, and steady, calculated growth—including cruise sales and group tours—has taken it to the $150 million level today. Azumano is consistently ranked by *Business Travel Survey* as one of the top 100 travel agencies in the nation.

Transcending Parochialism

George Azumano and Sho Dozono are such passionate advocates for the "internationalization" of Portland that most local residents would be amazed to know that international travel has never represented more than about two percent of the company's business—with Asia accounting for less than a third of that.

While it's true that Azumano profits as a wholesale broker for the international flights of airlines including United, Northwest, and Delta, Dozono says that his objectives in promoting an international perspective are pursued with a far larger mission than selling plane tickets.

"Internationalism is a banner issue for us," explains Dozono, "but it's never been about money. George and I both believe that it is important for the community to view itself in the context of a global perspective. Our international connections contribute significantly to the quality of life and the positive business environment that has led to Portland becoming a world-class city. The long-term health of our economy here depends on us—the citizens and the business community—thinking like major world players. If we keep a global perspective it will enhance our ability to remain economically competitive. It's all about transcending parochialism."

Through the years, Dozono and Azumano have volunteered a great deal of time and leadership in service to the community, striving to keep that global view alive and vital.

TECHNOLOGY HAS GREATLY CHANGED THE TRAVEL INDUSTRY DURING THE PAST DECADE AND AZUMANO HAS MADE SURE IT STAYS ON THE CUTTING EDGE. ITS WEB SITE, WWW.AZUMANOTRAVEL.COM, EARNED A TRAVELAGE WEST "TRENDSETTER" AWARD FOR USER-FRIENDLINESS AND DEPTH OF CONTENT. THE SITE OFFERS SEPARATE "CENTERS" FOR LEISURE AND CORPORATE TRAVEL.

AZUMANO HAS CARVED A SIZEABLE NICHE IN THE EXPANDING CRUISE MARKET WITH A DEDICATED OPERATION, CRUISES BY AZUMANO, AND MASTER CRUISE COUNSELORS WHOSE EXPERTISE HAS IMPRESSED CLIENTS FAR AND WIDE AND EARNED THE COMPANY A LOYAL FOLLOWING. PICTURED: CHARLOTTE HVAL, MANAGER.

In 1984, Azumano convinced executives at Fuji Television, one of Japan's leading networks, to produce an Oregon-based television drama that was frequently described as the Japanese version of "Little House on the Prairie."

"From Oregon With Love" was filmed in Central Oregon and ran for three years. It was a story that chronicled the adventures of a Japanese boy coming to live with his expatriate uncle's family in a small Oregon farming community. The show, which starred one of Japan's leading actors, became wildly successful in Japan, spurring a burst of tourist travel and Japanese documentaries focusing on what life in Oregon was really like.

Dozono pointed out that the experience led to countless exchanges among public officials, school children, and business people. "It's difficult to measure the impact, but the show made Oregon a household word in Japan and took us a long way toward understanding each other and developing relationships between Oregon and our major international trading partner," he said.

Azumano has served as past president of the Japan-America Society of Oregon, the Oregon Nikkei (Japanese-American) Legacy Center, the Governor's Tourism Council, and the Japanese Ancestral Society, and he is a lifetime trustee of Willamette University.

Dozono is a member of the International Trade Commission, has chaired the Portland Metropolitan Chamber of Commerce, and has served on the board of Portland State University Foundation, the Portland Art Museum, and the Portland Public Schools Foundation. He is past president and board member of the Portland/Oregon Visitors Association and has served on the Port of Portland Board of Commissioners. Nationally, Dozono has received recognition as a delegate to the White House Conference on Travel and Tourism. Most recently, he has led the effort to bring the Olympic Torch to Portland.

One of Azumano's most creative ventures caught the imagination of the entire country of Japan and probably has done more than any other single activity to raise the awareness of Oregon in that country.

Back To The Beginning

While it's true that the world has become smaller and the Azumano agency larger, there is a constant that sets the tone for all those who work there: George Azumano. Call him icon, legend, founder—he'll reject any of those terms as much too grandiose—he's a humble man. But it's clear that he continues to be the moral compass of the organization. Portland born and the son of Japanese immigrants who owned a grocery store in the city's Albina neighborhood—George's story is important because it's also the story of Portland's Asian experience.

George's parents came to the United States from Japan in 1917. Shortly after they arrived, his father became ill. His 22-year-old mother, determined to hold the family together, learned English, ran the family grocery store, and impressed upon her two children—George and a sister—the importance of studying hard and pursuing a good education.

George graduated from Jefferson High School and went on to earn a degree from the University of Oregon. Fate, however, delayed the launch of his professional career when his family, like thousands of other Japanese Americans, was forcibly uprooted during World War II and placed in a "relocation center." George reflects on the experience and recalls that literally thousands of Japanese volunteered to enlist despite the relocation, to show allegiance to the United States. "…and we left a legacy of bravery," he proudly recalls.

When the war ended and he returned to Portland, the experience—along with the hard-working example his mother had set—left George with a strong determination to succeed. He became an insurance agent, serving many Oregonians of Japanese descent. In 1948 when the U. S. government first allowed Japanese Americans to return to their homeland, older clients began to approach their trusted agent for help with the necessary passport documentation.

Travel arrangements were a logical extension of the help George was entrusted to provide and as time went on, a travel business grew steadily alongside his insurance operation. Most made the journey to Japan in those days by steamship, but George recalls that he sold his first airplane ticket in 1948 to an apple grower from Hood River. By the time the early '50s rolled around, airline travel replaced ocean transportation for the most part.

It was the first of many changes.

In 1988 George handed the reins to son-in-law Sho Dozono, who had been with the company since 1976 and who took the business George had built to the next level. "I feel fortunate that I'm part of the organization," Azumano reflects. "Sho has made it a bigger and better company and I'm very proud of him."

Still coming to the office once a week—and finally enjoying some travel that he ironically never had time for before, Azumano adds, "Time has brought about many changes, but I'm proud of the fact that we've never become too big or too busy to care." ■

COMPANY ICON AND FOUNDER GEORGE AZUMANO REFLECTS ON HIS FIVE DECADES IN BUSINESS, "TIME HAS BROUGHT ABOUT MANY CHANGES, BUT I'M PROUD OF THE FACT THAT WE'VE NEVER BECOME TOO BIG OR TOO BUSY TO CARE."

GEORGE AZUMANO (LOWER RIGHT) LEADS A TOUR GROUP TO JAPAN IN THE EARLY 1950s.

DOUBLETREE HOTELS

With four hotels located conveniently throughout the greater metropolitan area, Doubletree Hotels offer many visitors their first taste of the warm hospitality for which Oregon is known. Doubletree serves as Portland's leading convention hotel and plays host to more Portland visitors than any other chain.

Doubletree Hotels are a member of the Hilton Hotel Family. The facilities feature all the services and amenities you'd expect of a first-class hotel. Each provides a variety of casual and fine dining opportunities. Meeting and banquet facilities and full-service catering departments ensure the success of events, conferences, and parties. With a reputation for excellent customer service, attentive Doubletree staff is experienced at welcoming both domestic and international visitors. Room accommodations include the latest technology designed to serve the needs of the business traveler. A complimentary shuttle connects each hotel with Portland International Airport

And whether the visit is for business or pleasure guests can participate in the Hilton Hhonors—a reward program that allows travelers to earn mileage points accepted by more than 30 airlines as well as free merchandise and services from virtually every major retail outlet.

As Portland's leading convention hotel chain, the Doubletree and its employees are proud of the contribution they make to the promotion Portland's tourism industry. Employees are active members of the community supporting literally hundreds of causes that support Portland's reputation for beauty and livability.

Doubletree Portland Lloyd Center

The Lloyd Center is the largest hotel of the Doubletree's Portland family. The hotel is within walking distance of the Oregon Convention Center, the Rose Garden Arena, and Memorial Coliseum—the venues for Portland's largest convention, entertainment, and sports events. The MAX Light Rail system runs directly from the hotel to Portland's central business, shopping, and entertainment districts. Directly across the street is the expansive Lloyd Center Shopping Mall—the largest in Oregon.

For meetings and special events, the hotel offers 38,000 square feet of flexible meeting space, including 18 separate rooms, an exhibit hall, and four ballrooms. Professional staff can handle all needs including technical specifications and specialty catering.

The hotel's 476 guestrooms and suites are bright and airy. A swimming pool and exercise room is available for the enjoyment of guests. Two restaurants include the Coffee Garden—perfect for breakfast, lunch, or a bistro-style dinner. For microbrews and Mexican Fare, Eduardo's Margarita Grill is a popular stop.

Doubletree Portland Downtown

The Downtown Portland Doubletree is located just seven blocks from Portland's city center, close to downtown attractions and only 25 minutes from the airport. Oregon Zoo, Portland State University, Oregon Health Sciences University, and Waterfront Park are all within easy driving distance. Each of the 235 guestrooms provides full amenities and the hotel features a gift shop, fax, mail, and packaging handling.

The meeting and banquet facilities include eight separate rooms totaling 6,200 square feet. Professional conference specialists will take care of all needs including catering banquets for up to 350 people.

The Cityside Restaurant features fresh Northwest specialties and guests can find plenty of fun afterwards at the spirited Club Max. An exercise center and swimming pool are also available for guests to enjoy.

Doubletree Jantzen Beach And Columbia River Hotels

The Doubletree offers two hotels situated adjacent to each other on the scenic Columbia River at the south end of the I-5 Interstate bridge. Both hotels are just ten minutes from downtown Portland and 15 minutes away from Portland International Airport. The location makes them a convenient home base for trips to the Columbia River Gorge, the Oregon Coast, or downtown business calls. Five golf courses are located nearby as well as great shopping at Jantzen Beach Mall.

For larger events, the proximity of the two hotels allows groups to tap the resources of both facilities conveniently.

Situated west of Interestate-5 is the Columbia River Doubletree includes 352 spacious guestrooms including eight suites.

For meeting and events, 22,000 square feet of flexible meeting space offers boardroom, meeting rooms, and ballrooms, full-service catering, complete in-house audio-visual equipment, and an experienced convention services staff. Guests and local residents savor unique Northwest cuisine and river views at the newly remodeled Brickstones Restaurant and enjoy billiards and entertainment at the Brickstones Bar. Casual all-day dining is available at the Coffee Garden.

On the east side of I-5 is the Doubletree Jantzen Beach with 320 deluxe guest rooms including 24 suites, and all the amenities expected of a first-class hotel…plus a boat dock and heliopad.

Complete meeting facilities include 16 meeting rooms totaling 34,113 square feet with two river-view ballrooms and outside deck.

The Hayden Island Steakhouse offers prime beef entrees and the Coffee Garden is open all day for casual dining. Maxi's Lounge is a popular entertainment and dancing club for guests and locals. A swimming pool, hot tub, tennis courts, and fitness center offer options for the fitness enthusiast.

And then there are those chocolate chip cookies! Whether you visit for business or pleasure, all Portland Doubletree Hotels welcome guests with freshly baked chocolate chip cookies—a symbol of the warmth and hospitality that sets them apart. ■

METROPOLITAN EXPOSITION RECREATION COMMISSION

The Metropolitan Exposition-Recreation Commission (MERC) is a seven-member commission that manages, develops, and promotes the region's public assembly facilities including the Oregon Convention Center, the Portland Center for the Performing Arts (PCPA), and the Portland Metropolitan Exposition Center. The commission operates these regional facilities on behalf of Metro, the area's regional government. The MERC offices are located at the Oregon Convention Center.

Portland Center for the Performing Arts

The Portland Center for the Performing Arts (PCPA) is a collection of landmark theatres and performance halls situated in the city's "Bright Lights District" in downtown Portland. Comprised of Keller Auditorium, the Arlene Schnitzer Concert Hall, and the New Theatre Building (which houses the Newmark and Delores Winningstad Theatres and Brunish Hall) the PCPA is the cultural heart of the city and region. These five venues host more than 1,000 performances annually with attendance in excess of one million people—making PCPA one of the most active cultural centers in the nation. Dance companies, touring Broadway shows, lecture series, and musical performances featuring nationally known artists as well as local talent provide audiences with a rich array of quality cultural attractions.

Portland Metropolitan Exposition Center

The Portland Metropolitan Exposition Center—commonly known as the Expo Center—is the region's largest consumer and trade show venue of its kind. Expo Center is the site for a multitude of public shows and exhibitions including antique, auto, boat, home and garden shows, swap meets, and special events. Located just freeway minutes north of downtown Portland, the popularity of the exhibition and meeting facility has spurred an ambitious modernization and expansion program in recent years. Expo has opened two premiere exhibit halls since 1997, the most recent building opening in April 2001. These contemporary buildings provide modern exhibition conveniences and services, and offer 180,000 square feet of column free exhibit space. A new commercial kitchen and meeting rooms have increased the service offerings available at the facility. Expo Center offers 333,000 square feet of exhibition space and 2,500 parking

spaces on a 60-acre campus. Tri-Met's Interstate Max light rail service will provide public transit service to Expo Center beginning 2004. Expo Center's shining modern structures provide a stark contrast to the livestock buildings that long-time residents may recall from the past.

The Oregon Convention Center

The Oregon Convention Center, which completes the triumvirate of public facilities, is the centerpiece of the region's convention and trade show industry. Located on the East Bank of the Willamette River in the city center, the stunning structure with its trademark twin glass towers has won national acclaim for its design. Business at the Convention Center generates significant economic benefits for the community, state, and region, pumping about $475 million into the region's economy each year and supporting 7,900 local jobs. The full vision for the Convention Center will be realized in the year 2003 when a 405,000-square-foot expansion will be added to the 500,000-square-foot structure that was originally opened in 1990. ∎

ROSE GARDEN ARENA
PORTLAND TRAIL BLAZERS

I f you live in Portland you know what we're talking about and if you're new to our fair city you're about to find out. Find out about what? BLAZERMANIAAAA! Portland loves its basketball team. And that might explain why the Portland Trail Blazers have become one of the most innovative, diverse, and successful franchises in all of professional sports.

Since 1970 when Portland's Harry Glickman was granted an expansion franchise by the NBA Board of Governors, the Blazer story has unfolded to include an NBA Championship, two near misses, and the opening of one of the nation's most impressive new arenas–the award winning Rose Garden.

Only seven years after the team was franchised, it did what only one other team in the history of the league has done: win a championship in its first post-season appearance. Portland fans saw it coming and two months before the playoffs, began to pack capacity crowds into Memorial Coliseum–setting a record for sell out crowds that continued for almost 20 years. On June 6, 1977 when the Blazers came from behind to win the NBA Championship the Rose City went into a frenzy. Hundreds of thousands of Blazermaniacs took to the streets to celebrate Portland's win over Philadelphia and the term "Blazermania" became a part of the sports lexicon from coast to coast.

In 1988, Paul G. Allen, cofounder of Microsoft, purchased the Trail Blazers. Allen has made good on a promise to give the fans a winning and exciting team. During his tenure, the Blazers have won more than 60 percent of their games and continued a 19 consecutive year play-off streak after the 2000-01 season, which is the second longest in the history of professional sports.

The opening of the Blazers new arena–the Rose Garden–in 1995 was another landmark on the Blazers trail of success. Built by Paul Allen, the Rose Garden is a state-of-the-art 20,000 capacity arena that offers a brilliant array of world-class entertainment features. With the largest seating capacity of any arena on the West Coast, the Rose Garden also is home to the Portland Fire of the WNBA, the Portland Winter Hawks of the Western Hockey League, and attracts the hottest concerts, family shows, and sporting events.

The Rose Garden is the centerpiece of a 32-acre campus, which includes the Veteran's Memorial Coliseum, offices, restaurants, and an inviting public plaza.

The Blazers efforts in the community to improve the lives of children and the people who support them may explain why the team is so loved. The Blazers have been recognized for their contributions to groups including SMART–Start Making A Reader Today; Boys & Girls Clubs of Portland; Police Activities League, YMCA, Salvation Army, and Self-Enhancement, Inc.–a program for inner city youth.

In 1999, the Blazers won the National Points of Light Foundation award for excellence in corporate community service, the first time the award went to a sports franchise. Team and staff are active in the community supporting a broad spectrum of programs, the centerpiece of which is the Blazers Community Builders.

As one Blazer executive put it, "Serving others helps us all to play for something bigger than ourselves."

With attitude like that, fans can count on every season being a winning season for the Portland Trail Blazers and their community. ∎

THE ROSE GARDEN IS ONE OF PORTLAND'S SKYLINE LANDMARKS. THE AWARD-WINNING VENUE IS HOME TO THE BLAZERS, PORTLAND FIRE OF THE WNBA, AND THE WINTERHAWKS OF THE WESTERN HOCKEY LEAGUE, AS WELL AS CONCERTS, FAMILY SHOWS, AND OTHER SPORTING EVENTS.

SOME OUTRAGEOUS FANS CHEER ON THE PORTLAND TRAIL BLAZERS. BLAZERS FANS ARE OFTEN TOUTED AROUND THE NBA AS THE BEST FANS IN THE LEAGUE.

ENTERPRISE INDEX

Adventist Medical Center
10123 Southeast Market Street
Portland, Oregon 97216
Phone: 503-257-2500
Fax: 503-261-6628
E-mail: pamarketing@ah.org
www.adventisthealth.com
Page 196

**AmberGlen Business Center/
Birtcher Commercial Development Group**
1600 Northwest Compton Drive, Suite 106
Beaverton, Oregon 97006
Phone: 503-690-1025
Fax: 503-690-1444
E-mail: knickerson@birtcher.com
www.amberglen.com
Page 184

Azumano Travel
Executive Offices:
320 Southwest Stark Street, Suite 600
Portland, Oregon 97204
Phone: 503-223-6245
          800-777-2018
Fax: 503-294-6474
E-mail: info@azumano.com
www.azumanotravel.com
Pages 202-205

Becker Capital Management
1211 Southwest Fifth Avenue, Suite 2185
Portland, Oregon 97204
Phone: 503-223-1720
Fax: 503-223-3624
E-mail: jmcaninch@beckercap.com
www.beckercap.com
Page 162

Bonneville Power Administration
PO Box 3621
905 Northeast 11th Avenue
Portland, Oregon 97208
Phone: 503-230-5109
Fax: 503-230-4019
E-mail: crstenehjem@bpa.gov
Pages 152-153

Centennial Bank
One Southwest Columbia Street, Suite 900
Portland, Oregon 97258
Phone: 503-973-5556
Fax: 503-973-5557
E-mail: bscott@centennialbank.com
www.centennialbank.com
Page 164

Doubletree Hotels
Phone: 800-222-8733
E-mail: janelle_cram@hilton.com
www.doubletree.com
Pages 206-207

Group Mackenzie
0690 Southwest Bancroft Street
PO Box 69039
Portland, Oregon 97201-0039
Phone: 503-224-9560
Fax: 503-228-1285
E-mail: info@grpmack.com
www.groupmackenzie.com
Pages 180-181

IBM
15450 Southwest Koll Parkway
Beaverton, Oregon 97006
Phone: 800-426-4968
www.ibm.com
Pages 136-137

IDT (Integrated Device Technology)
3131 Northeast Brookwood Parkway
Hillsboro, Oregon 97124
Phone: 503-693-4696
Fax: 503-693-3595
www.idt.com
Pages 132-135

Kaiser Permanente
500 Northeast Multnomah, Suite 100
Portland, Oregon 97232
Phone: 503-813-2000 (option 4)
Fax: 503-813-4235
E-mail: sharon.e.o'keefe@kp.org
www.kp.org/nw
Page 198

Metropolitan Exposition Recreation Commission
777 Northeast Martin Luther King Jr. Boulevard
Portland, Oregon 97232
PO Box 2746
Portland, Oregon 97208
Phone: 503-731-7800
Fax: 503-731-7870
www.merc-facilities.org
Page 208

Nike, Inc.
One Bowerman Drive
Beaverton, Oregon 97005-6453
Phone: 503-671-6453
Fax: 503-671-6300
www.nike.com
Pages 144-145

Norris, Beggs & Simpson
121 Southwest Morrison, Suite 200
Portland, Oregon 97204
Phone: 503-223-7181
Fax: 503-273-0256
www.nbsrealtors.com
Pages 182-183

NW Natural
220 Northwest 2nd Avenue
Portland, Oregon 97209
Phone: 503-226-4211
Fax: 503-721-2539
www.nwnatural.com
Pages 148-149

Office Suites and Services
1100 Southwest Sixth Avenue, Suite 1212
Portland, Oregon 97204
Phone: 503-223-3201
Fax: 503-222-4429
E-mail: gamiller@office-suites-services.com
www.office-suites-services.com
Page 172

Oregon Health & Science University
3181 Southwest Sam Jackson Park Road
Portland, Oregon 97201-3098
Phone: 503-494-8311
www.ohsu.edu
Pages 188-191

PacifiCorp
825 Northeast Multnomah, Suite 2000
Portland, Oregon 97232
Phone: 503-813-5000
E-mail: webmaster@pacificorp.com
www.pacificorp.com
Page 155

PG&E National Energy Group
1400 Southwest 5th Avenue, #900
Portland, Oregon 97201
Phone: 503-833-4000
Fax: 503-833-4913
www.neg.pge.com
Page 154

Portland General Electric
121 Southwest Salmon Street
Portland, Oregon 97204
Phone: 503-228-6322
Fax: 503-612-3742
E-mail: customer_service@pgn.com
www.portlandgeneral.com
Pages 150-151

Portland Metropolitan Chamber of Commerce
221 Northwest Second Avenue
Portland, Oregon 97209-3999
Phone: 503-552-5632
Fax: 503-228-5126
E-mail: news@pdxchamber.org
www.pdxchamber.org
Pages 158-159

Portland Veterans Affairs Medical Center
3710 Southwest US Veterans Hospital Road
PO Box 1034
Portland, Oregon 97207
Phone: 503-220-8262
Fax: 503-273-5319
Pages 192-195

Providence Health System
1235 Northeast 47th Avenue
Portland, Oregon 97213
Phone: 503-215-4860
Fax: 503-215-4703
www.providence.org
Page 197

Purdy Corporation
13201 North Lombard
Portland, Oregon 97203
Phone: 503-286-8217
Fax: 503-286-5336
E-mail: davidh@purdycorp.com
www.purdycorp.com
Pages 142-143

Rose Garden Arena/Portland Trail Blazers
One Center Court, Suite 200
Portland, Oregon 97227
Phone: 503-234-9291
Fax: 503-736-2194
E-mail: blazersfeedback@ripcity.com
www.blazers.com
www.rosequarter.com
Page 209

Russell Development Company, Inc.
200 Southwest Market Street, Suite 678
Portland, Oregon 97201
Phone: 503-228-2500
Fax: 503-228-3204
E-mail: sheryl_scali@cushwake.com
Pages 176-179

SRG Partnership, PC
621 Southwest Morrison Street, Suite 200
Portland, Oregon 97205
Phone: 503-222-1917
Fax: 503-294-0272
E-mail: srg@srgpartnership.com
www.srgpartnership.com
Pages 168-171

TRANSFAC
815 Southwest 2nd, #300
Portland, Oregon 97208
Phone: 503-226-3493
　　　　800-222-2307
Fax: 503-226-2065
E-mail: sales@TRANSFAC.com
www.TRANSFAC.com
Page 163

Tripwire, Inc.
326 Southwest Broadway, 3rd Floor
Portland, Oregon 97205
Phone: 503-276-7500
Fax: 503-223-0182
www.tripwire.com
Page 138

U.S. Trust
The River Forum, Suite 450
4380 Southwest Macadam Avenue
Portland, Oregon 97201
Phone: 503-228-2300
Fax: 503-228-1724
E-mail: info.pnw@ustrust.com
www.ustrust.com
Page 160

West Coast Bank
Corporate Office:
5335 Meadows Road, Suite 201
Lake Oswego, Oregon 97035
Phone: 503-684-0884
Fax: 503-684-0781
www.wcb.com
Page 165

The William C. Earhart Company, Inc.
PO Box 4148
3140 Northeast Broadway
Portland, Oregon 97208
Phone: 503-282-5581
Fax: 503-284-9386
E-mail: cgladstone@wcearhart.com
Page 161

WRG Design, Inc.
5415 Southwest Westgate Drive
Portland, Oregon 97221
Phone: 503-419-2500
Fax: 503-419-2600
E-mail: rbn@wrgd.com
www.wrgd.com
Page 185

BIBLIOGRAPHY & ACKNOWLEDGEMENTS

Publications
Oregon Business, July 1, 2001
Oregon Health, Spring 2001
The Business Journal, Portland Metro Area Shopping Centers supplement
Portland Guide Discovering Oregon, Summer 2000
The *Oregonian,* March 15, 2001
Oregon Business, Oregon Industrial & Business Parks Guide 2002 supplement

Web sites
Bridges–http://www.bizave.com/portland/bridges/
Bridge Pedal–http://www.bizave.com/portland/bridges/
Do Jump! Extremely Physical Theatre–http://www.dojump.org/html/main.htm
Kaiser Permanente–www.KaiserPermanente.org
Lewis & Clark College–www.LClark.edu
Marylhurst University–http://www.marylhurst.edu/home.html
Multnomah Falls Lodge–http://www.ohwy.com/or/m/multfalo.htm
Oregonian Newspaper–http://www.oregonlive.com/cgi, bin/printer/printer.cgi
Oregon Symphony–www.orsymphony.org
PGE Park–http://www.pgepark.com, http://www.pgepark.com/about/history.cfm
Pittock Mansion–http://www.mediaforte.com/pittock/history.htm; http://www.ohwy.com/or/p/pittockm.htm
Portland–http://www.el.com/To/Portland/
Portland Development Commission–http://www.portlanddev.org/
Portland Institute for Contemporary Art–http://www.pica.org/htdocs/
Portland Metropolitan Chamber of Commerce–Portland Opera–http://www.portlandopera.org/education/education.html
Portland Parks–http://www.parks.ci.portland.or.us/services/urbanforestry.htm
Portland Rose Festival–www.RoseFestival.org
Portland State University–http://www.pdx.edu/
Portland Streetcar–http://www.pportlandstreetcar.org/index.html
Portland Winter Hawks–http://www.winterhawks.com/
Procession of the Species–http://www.earthandspirit.org
Reed College–http://www.reed.edu
Tri-Met–http://www.tri-met.org
Tryon Creek State Park–http://www.ohwy.com/or/t/tryoncrk.htm; http://www.upa.pdx.edu/CWSP/WATSHED/tryon/tryon.htm
Tygres Heart Shakespeare Company–http://www.tygresheart.org/mission.cfm
University of Portland–http://www.up.edu/
Water Treatment Plant–http://www.enviro.ci.portland.or.us/cbwtp.htm
Willamette River–http://www.planning.ci.portland.or.us/River_site/Layers.htm
    http://www.portlandchamber.com/visiting/see_and_do.htm; http://www.portlandchamber.com/visiting/Family_Adventures.htm

The editorial coordinator and publisher would like to thank the following people and organizations that contributed information to this book:

Artists Repertory Theatre–Loriann Thye
Chinatown Gate–POVA
City of Portland–Lee Barrett
Crystal Springs Rhododendron Garden–Rita
Do Jump! Extremely Physical Theatre–Howie Bierbaum
Fujitsu–Marla Barney
Intel Corporation–Bill MacKenzie
Kaiser Permanente–Mike
Kids on the Block–Kristine
Leach Botanical Garden–Jan
Lewis & Clark College–Mr. Shannon Smith
Marylhurst University–John McDonald-O'Lear
Mt. Hood Community College–Janet Brayson
Oaks Park–Mary Beth Coffey
Oregon Health & Science University–Caryn Ruch
Oregon Museum of Science and Industry–Karen Caine
Oregon Children's Theatre–Jill Baum, Sharon Martell
Oregon Ballet Theatre–Barry Beach, Julia Sheridan
Oregon Golf Association–Kevin
Oregon Humane Society–Kathy Neely
Oregon Zoo–Bill LaMarsh
Orenco Station–Judi Bost
PGE Park–Mike Siriani, Jan Davis
PICA–Victoria Frey

Pittock Mansion
Port of Portland–Aaron Ellis
Portland Art Museum–Beth Sorensen, Jean Zondervan
Portland Center for the Performing Arts–Judy Siemssen
Portland Institute for Contemporary Art–Victoria Frey
Portland Japanese Garden
Portland Opera–Laura Bartroff
Portland Parks–Jennifer
Portland Police–Terri
Portland Rose Festival
Portland State University–Jeanie-Marie Price, Jean Tuomi
Portland Winter Hawks–Kelley Robinett
POVA–Carlos, Arietta (and several others)
Procession of the Species–Pam, Deborah, Gretchen
Providence Hospital–Dianne E. McConkey
Queen Anne Victorian Mansion–Katy
Reed College–Laurie Lindquist
St. James Lutheran Church–Barbara
Tri-Met–Janene Riemer, Mary Fetsch
Tygres Heart Shakespeare–Marci E. Cochran
University of Portland–Mary Scroggins
Vintage Trolley
Willamette Shore Trolley
World Forestry Center-Roxie

BIOGRAPHIES

Jann Mitchell

As a Portland journalist for thirty-five years, Jann Mitchell has seen all sides of the city–including life aboard a houseboat on rural Sauvie Island, forgoing television in favor of living in peace with the wildlife around her. She writes articles about simplifying, decorating, and relationships and books–*Home Sweeter Home: Creating a Haven of Simplicity and Spirit* sells in different languages around the world. She's a sought-after lecturer on the simple life, and divides her time between Portland and Stockholm, Sweden. The South Park Blocks in fall and the Japanese Garden are her favorite Portland places. Those interested can reach Jann at jannmmitchell@aol.com.

Lucy Z. Martin, APR

Lucy Z. Martin, APR, is credited with starting the health-care marketing profession in Oregon nearly twenty-five years ago. She's counseled more than fifty hospitals, insurers, physician practices, and clinics, both in the allopathic (MD) and in the complementary disciplines. She is a frequent keynote speaker and policy strategist to health-care organizations and holds numerous distinctions and honors.

Dick Montgomery

Dick Montgomery is a descendent of Dr. William H. Willson who landed at Fort Vancouver in 1837, and went on to help steer the Oregon Territory toward statehood and establish the city of Salem, Oregon. Dick's father was a noted Northwest author and book reviewer. With this heritage it is not surprising Dick has become a student of Oregon history. His expertise lies in the field of transportation. During his forty-year career, Dick been a journalist and public relations executive representing bus companies, railroads, truck lines, docks and ports. He retired in 1995 after nearly twenty years with the Port of Portland as marine public affairs manager and editor of the Port's internationally-circulated *Portside* news magazine. He now owns Montgomery Marine Communications and represents a number of transportation industry clients.

Russ Nelson

Russ Nelson is a Portland area writer and publisher whose pioneer family came to Oregon shortly after the Civil War. He holds Masters Degrees from Marshall University in Huntington, West Virginia, and the University of New Hampshire in Durham, New Hampshire. His writing career includes free-lance magazine writing, newspaper reporting, and advertising. Russ worked on the staffs of *Oregon Business* and *Oregon* magazines, and served as publisher of *Western Investor* and *Barter Age* magazines. He taught as a National Teacher Corp volunteer in Appalachia, and as a Teaching Assistant at the University of New Hampshire. He also taught (as a volunteer) at the Portsmouth New Hampshire Naval Prison, and closed his teaching career as a secondary school teacher in Oregon.

Kyle Ritchey-Noll

Kyle Ritchey-Noll was the executive director of the Oregon Council of the AeA, the industry's leading trade group, from 1988-2000. During that time, she helped lead the industry through the challenges and opportunities that led to the transformation of high-tech from a start-up industry to Oregon's leading economic engine. Ritchey-Noll continues to work with Oregon's technology industry as a community relations and public affairs consultant. A native Oregonian, she lives in Wilsonville with her husband and two daughters.

Richard G. Reiten

Richard G. Reiten joined Northwest Natural in January of 1996 as President and Chief Operating Officer. A year later, he was named President and Chief Executive Officer; then, in September 2000, Chairman of the Board. Prior to 1996, his experience included serving as President and Chief Operating Officer of Portland General Electric, Director of the Oregon Economic Development Department, Chair for Development of the State of Oregon Strategic Plan, and President, Chief Executive Officer and Director of Nicolai Company.

Having earned a BA in Business Administration from the University of Washington and completed the Executive, and Board of Directors Programs at Stanford School of Business, Mr. Reiten's skill in dealing with the international business community led to his appointment in 1988 to the Inter Governmental Advisory Council to the U.S. Trade Representative in Washington, D.C. Actively involved in the community, serving on numerous boards and working with civic organizations, Reiten resides in Portland with his wife, Jean. They have three grown children: Patrick, Christopher and Holly Lynne.

George Taylor

George Taylor grew up in the farmlands of west central Michigan, an experience that influenced his life and writing. He has had a lifelong involvement in the arts, which manifested itself in acting and stage directing. In 1978, Taylor realized a long-standing dream by moving to Portland. He believes strongly in the transforming power of the arts and sees them as an essential part of life. Taylor has written and edited publications for the Oregon Arts Commission and served on the Commission's theatre grants panel from 1996 through 1998. He is a member of the Arts and Culture Committee of the Portland City Club, serving as co-chair in 1995 and 1996. He currently serves on the board of one Portland music organization and as president of the board of a Portland theatre company.

Has been writing professionally for about the last thirty years, including fourteen years as creative director of a Portland advertising agency. He and his wife, Edie, live in Beaverton.

Kathy Dimond Watson

Kathy Watson writes and consults for and about business and government on economic and business development, communications, and public policy issues. For fun, she also writes about food, travel, and life. She is the former Editor-in-Chief of *Oregon Business* magazine and editorial director of *Oregon Business Media*. Kathy joined the magazine in 1992, rebuilding both its content and its readership, and played an active role in creating the custom publishing division, growing it to the largest custom publisher in the Pacific Northwest.

Ms. Watson has been involved in business, government, and politics in Oregon for twenty years. She served as press secretary to the State Senate Democratic Caucus, and as communications director for the state Labor Commissioner and the state Economic Development Department, as well as press secretary to the Mayor of Portland. She and her husband, Stuart, live in Hood River, Oregon.

Stu Watson

A veteran of twenty-four years with Pacific Northwest newspapers and magazines, Stu Watson has been honored by professional organizations for his writing style, including columns and humor. After helping set up the editorial operations at two startup interactive multimedia companies in Denver, Colorado, Watson in 1997 started his own company helping business clients capture in words their singular and compelling stories. Stu's list of clients includes Pacific Bell, Ameritech, Arthur Andersen, CA1 Services, and the Oregon University System. He and wife, Kathy Watson, now operate their similar business efforts as Watson x 2. As his own boss, he is happy to grant himself time off to ski, windsurf, hike, camp, paddle, snowshoe, and fish in and around Portland.

Maggi White

Maggi White has been tracing Portland's economic growth since 1973, when she founded the *Downtowner*, which focused on the downtown hub, as well as during her founding of another Portland publication, *Ourtown*, in 1995. She has written a column all those years, talking about the city, its people, and a variety of topics from books to philosophy. White has watched the city grow from one tall building, to a dramatic skyline that shows off lighted bridges and a shimmering, now active waterfront. She has been editor and publisher of the two publications mentioned above, is a past president of the Downtown Retail Council, and is honorary member of the Jazz Society of Oregon, which has helped make Portland a lively music scene.